Aussie STEM Stars

JOHN LONG
Fossil hunter

JOHN LONG
Fossil hunter

Story told by DANIELLE CLODE

Aussie STEM Stars series
Published by Wild Dingo Press
Melbourne, Australia
books@wilddingopress.com.au
wilddingopress.com.au

This work was first published by Wild Dingo Press 2021
Text copyright © Danielle Clode

The moral right of the author has been asserted.

Reproduction and communication for educational purposes:
The Australian *Copyright Act 1968* (the Act) allows a maximum of
one chapter or 10% of the pages of this work, whichever is the greater, to be
reproduced and/or communicated by an educational institution for its educational
purposes provided that the educational institution (or the body that administers it)
has given a remuneration to Copyright Agency under the Act.
For details of the Copyright Agency licence for educational institutions contact:

Copyright Agency
Level 11, 66 Goulburn Street
Sydney NSW 2000
Email: info@copyright.com.au

Reproduction and communication for other purposes:
Except as permitted under the *Copyright Act 1968*, no part of this book may be
reproduced, stored in a retrieval system, or transmitted in any form or by any
means without prior written permission.
All inquiries should be made to the Publisher, Wild Dingo Press.

Cover Design: Gisela Beer
Illustrations: Mirjana Segan
Series Editor: Catherine Lewis
Printed in Australia

Clode, Danielle 1968-, author.
John Long: Fossil hunter / Danielle Clode

A catalogue record for this
book is available from the
National Library of Australia

ISBN: 9781925893687 (paperback)
ISBN: 9781925893618 (epdf)
ISBN: 9781925893625 (epub)

*A detailed knowledge of the past
can cool the rising heat of the future.*
– John Long

Disclaimer
This work has been developed in collaboration with Professor John Long. The utmost care has been taken to respectfully portray, as accurately as memory allows, the events and the stories of all who appear in this work. The publishers assume no liability or responsibility for unintended inaccuracies but would be pleased to rectify at the earliest opportunity any omissions or errors brought to their notice.

Contents

1. A mystery from the quarry   1
2. Fossil fever   8
3. Meeting the professor   15
4. Underwater worlds   23
5. Meeting the big boss   33
6. A new school   42
7. Camping chaos   54
8. Karate kid   68
9. You'll never get a job   82
10. Into the West   99
11. Fossils in the spotlight   116
12. A cold shock and a fishy family   131
13. Life in LA   148
14. Future of fossils   157
     Glossary   165
     About Danielle Clode   167

1

A mystery from the quarry

John did up his coat and rubbed his arms as he got out of the car. It was an early spring morning in the hills outside Melbourne and it was freezing. Des's dad, Mr Matthews, had picked him up from home when it was still dark and they'd driven for an hour to get here. The sun was coming up over the rolling hills now, but there wasn't much to see.

Some cows grazed among scraggy bushes. Magpies warbled in the trees. A small creek flowed through the paddock. Over the other side, reeds grew around a dip in the ground. It was the last place you'd expect to find anything exciting.

Mr Matthews hoisted a heavy bag of chisels and hammers over his shoulder, picked up a large crowbar and slammed the car boot shut.

'Follow me, boys,' he said, grinning cheerfully.

He held up the wire fence for the boys to climb through and they headed down to the creek. The rising sun sent wisps of steam from the paddocks into the frosty air. Des and John left dark footprints in the damp grass as they ran ahead, jumping over the uneven ground.

Des sat next to John in their Grade 2 class at All Hallows Primary School in Balwyn. It was a small basic school run by the Sisters of St Joseph. It had four mixed-grade classes in an old church and a temporary building. The yard was concrete and bitumen. Good for ball games but bad for grazing knees. In summer the yard was hot and the little cartons of milk given out to all the schoolkids at morning recess were already warm.

Des often came over to John's house at the top of Hilda Street after school. It was the perfect spot for launching billycarts or racing bikes. In summer, they cooled down in the backyard, squirting each other with the hose or throwing pots of water. There was a big oval nearby where they kicked the footy. Sometimes they caught tadpoles and golden bell frogs in the surrounding swamps and bushland.

Des and John often argued about their favourite football teams. Des barracked for Melbourne and John barracked for Collingwood, like his dad. When Melbourne narrowly beat Collingwood in the nail-biting 1964 Grand Final, John lost his threepence lunch money to Des. To make up for it, Des had invited John to come on a fossil-collecting trip to the Lilydale quarry with his dad.

As they headed across the open paddock, something large and dark suddenly swept across the back of John's head. Magpies are fierce protectors of their young and one of the nesting magpies was on the attack. It turned and dived again at John. He waved his arms and ran for cover under the trees by the creek. Des followed, waving a big stick to keep the bird away. As they headed across to the reedy hollow, the magpie retreated to its nest.

John's heart was racing. It wasn't from the magpie. It was from excitement. Today he was going to find a dinosaur.

Like most seven-year-old boys, John knew a lot about dinosaurs. He remembered nearly every word from the 50-pence copy of the *How and Why Book of Dinosaurs* his mum and dad had bought him. He'd read it so much it was nearly worn out.

'Here we are,' said Mr Matthews. 'The old quarry.'

'Did they dig this up looking for dinosaurs?' asked John.

'No,' said Mr Matthews, 'just for building stone.'

In the middle of the quarry long reeds grew around a dark pool of water. Tumbled boulders lay at the bottom of the dark grey rock walls.

If John was lucky, he might find a meat-eating *Tyrannosaurus rex*, a three-horned *Triceratops* or even a giant *Brontosaurus*.

> When John was small, not much was known about Australian dinosaurs. Most books were about American dinosaurs, like **Tyrannosaurus**, **Triceratops** and **Brontosaurus** (now known as **Apatosaurus**).

'Here, grab a hammer and start breaking open the rocks,' Des's dad instructed them.

He picked up a split rock to show John. It was flecked with orange inside, like paint.

'This is mudstone,' he said. 'Millions of years ago this was mud on the sea floor. Little creatures living there were buried in the mud. Now they've become **fossils**. These orange marks are the impressions of their remains. See, this one's a shell.'

John looked closely at the round orange blob in the rock. It didn't look like much. Then suddenly, he could see a fan shape. It looked a bit like a small clam shell.

Now that he knew what to look for, John started smashing up chunks of rock. It didn't take long before he found some orange marks.

He opened a rock with a series of orange raised ripples in the middle. It looked a bit like a flattened prawn tail. John showed Mr Matthews.

'It's a trilobite,' Mr Matthews said, smiling. 'This is the tail of a beetle-like creature that lived at the bottom of the sea about 400 million years ago. In those days, the sea covered all the land we're standing on.'

John was amazed. He tried to imagine the hills and farmland around him being at the bottom of the ocean. Four hundred million years was a really long time ago. He was thrilled with the idea that he was the first person ever to see the remains of this little animal.

They spent the rest of the day happily smashing away at rocks, with the sun warming their backs. At lunchtime, they devoured their sandwiches and cakes, washing them down with sweet orange cordial. Mr Matthews told them that most of the fossils here were the remains of small sea creatures from the bottom of the ocean. This didn't bother John. Maybe a dinosaur bone or tooth had been washed down a river and out to sea. If he looked hard enough, surely he'd find one.

From that moment on, John was hooked. He had caught fossil fever.

2

Fossil fever

When John got home, he couldn't wait to show his mum and dad his discoveries. First, he used an old toothbrush to scrub the dirt off the fossils. Then he put them in a box, labelled with where and when he'd found them.

Nothing he'd found looked remotely like a dinosaur, but he had found some mysterious fossils that even Mr Matthews couldn't identify.

He brought his treasures out to the kitchen where his mum was cooking dinner and sat next to his dad. His parents had both been at work and looked a bit tired.

'What've you got there, Johnny?' his dad asked him.

'They look interesting, dear,' said his mum as she stirred the pot on the stove, looking very elegant after work at the Balwyn Cinema, her long blonde hair in a bun. John's mum loved cooking.

She loved telling family stories too. She told great stories about John's much older brother Keith. John loved the story about Keith tightrope walking on the clothesline or teaching the neighbour's cocky to swear. Sometimes John's mum would tell him about his inventive Norwegian grandfather and his bravery in France during the First World War. Or when his great-grandfather sailed with the famous Norwegian explorer and scientist Fridtjof Nansen, who might have been a distant relative.

John's dad had a very different background. He had a lean build with fine features, much like John. His family was Irish and John's great-great-grandfather had made a fortune running the Sunshine Biscuit Factory (in Melbourne's western suburb of Sunshine) with the Latin motto *Labor Omnia Vincit* – meaning 'work conquers all'.

The fortune had disappeared by the time John's dad was growing up on the farm but there was still plenty of hard work. John's dad never talked about his childhood much or about his time in the army in New Guinea during the Second World War.

'What's this one, then?' asked his dad, picking up one of the fossils.

A long, curved orange line snaked across the rock, with what looked like little legs coming off the sides. Even Mr Matthews had been puzzled by this one and couldn't say what it was.

'It's a fossil centipede,' declared John, carefully writing the name on the box. Mr Matthews had told him that some of the fossils might be new species that didn't even have names. He picked up the trilobite he'd found. Maybe this was a new species, too, that no one had studied before.

> When scientists find new fossil species they draw, describe and name them. All organisms, living or extinct, have a **two-part scientific name.** The first name or *genus* is like our surnames – species share this name with their closest relatives. The second name is like our first name, which is used only for that one species. John's trilobite had not been named when he found it in 1964 but was described as *Acaste longisulcata* in 1968.

'Put them away now, love,' said John's mum, 'dinner's ready.'

Over dinner John's mum talked about her work. Usually, John looked forward to seeing the matinee for free every weekend while his mum worked at the cinema. But he wasn't as excited about the latest Godzilla movie as usual. All he could think about was his new fossil collection and how soon he could get back to the quarry to find more.

John's dad agreed to take the boys back to the quarry and on each trip they gathered more and more fossils. Sometimes they were lucky enough to find a trilobite head, rather than just the tail.

John's interest in fossils grew and grew. He began taking notes from library books and making long lists of animals he learnt about.

Sometimes he even drew pictures of them. He loved learning all their names and rolling them off his tongue.

John's mum was so proud of her 'dinosaur expert' that when a visitor arrived, she would call John to come and tell them what he knew.

'Go on, Johnny, say those prehistoric names for us.'

'*Pterodactylus, Brontosaurus, Tyrannosaurus, Triceratops, Stegosaurus,*' John would recite.

'What do you think of this one?' asked John one night after dinner. He showed his parents the fossil he'd just cleaned. It was only small, about a centimetre long, but it was thin and curved.

'Looks like a tooth,' his dad said.

John nodded and opened the page of his book to a drawing of a large plant-eating dinosaur known as *Iguanodon*.

'I think it's an *Iguanodon* tooth,' he said.

'Could be,' agreed his dad cautiously.

No one had ever found an *Iguanodon* tooth in Australia before. John wondered if this discovery would make him famous.

'You should ask someone at the Museum or the University,' suggested his mum.

'I'll ask one of the **geologists** at work,' his dad volunteered.

John's dad had originally trained as a tailor and was always the one who took up the hems on John's jeans. But after he left the army, he had worked in lots of different jobs. He drove trucks across the unsealed Nullarbor highway for a while and later worked in a chicken-plucking factory. By the time John was eight, his dad was working as a security guard at the head office of a big mining company in Collins Street, so he often talked to the geologists who worked there. One of them gave him the name of a professor at the University of Melbourne who might know about John's fossil.

That evening, John wrote a letter to the professor. He included a sketch of his magnificent dinosaur tooth – the first *Iguanodon* to be found in Australia. Sealing up the envelope, he stuck a stamp on it and posted it in the mailbox just down the street. And then he waited for an answer.

3

Meeting the professor

'John!' called his mum as he arrived home from school. 'There's a letter here for you.'

John excitedly opened the letter, with its university crest embossed at the top. It was a reply from Professor George Baker in the Geology Department.

The professor invited John to bring his specimens in to the department so he could have a closer look.

John was over the moon with excitement! He must have found something really amazing if a professor wanted to see his fossils.

'Can we go tomorrow, Dad?' he asked.

'We'll have to make an appointment, Johnny,' he said. 'Professors are busy people.'

Over the next few days, John studied his books on fossils, memorising the names of all the dinosaurs and making a detailed list of all of his specimens. He didn't want to look stupid in front of the professor.

When the big day finally came, John's dad drove into the city and parked the car near the university. They wandered in to look for the Geology Department. John was awestruck! There were so many large and grand old buildings, each labelled with their area of study: Zoology, Botany, Chemistry, Physics.

Eventually, they found the Geology Building and walked up the steps to the imposing entrance. John's dad told the receptionist they had an appointment with Professor Baker.

A few moments later the professor appeared, holding John's letter in his hand. He had a very friendly face and he smiled broadly when he saw John and his dad.

'So, this is Master John Long, eh,' he said warmly, shaking John's hand firmly. 'You've got your specimens with you, I see. Well then, let's have a look at them, shall we?'

'Yes, sir,' John replied nervously, clutching his precious shoebox of fossils tightly under one arm. He put the box down and took off the lid.

'I think this one is a dinosaur tooth,' John said, hastily. 'From an *Iguanodon*.'

'Well, well, that would be an interesting find, indeed,' the professor responded.

John unwrapped the specimen and carefully placed it in the palm of his hand. The professor looked at it closely, turning it over. John's heart was racing.

'Where did you say this came from?' the professor asked.

'Lilydale, sir. From the quarry on Edwards Road.'

'Ah, yes, I know the spot,' he said. 'We often take students there. Shall we have a look at our collections and see if we can solve the mystery?'

They walked along the corridor to a large room filled with glass-topped wooden cabinets displaying all sorts of fossils and rocks. Each one had a neatly typed label on it. John grinned at his dad, who

was standing quietly in the corner – he'd never seen such a big fossil collection before.

'Over here, John,' called the professor. 'See, here, these fossils all come from the Lilydale district. The rocks are from the Devonian Period, which was 360 million years ago. This was well before the first dinosaurs had appeared on the planet.'

John's heart sank. He had been so sure he'd found a dinosaur tooth. So what was it then? He scanned the orange fossils and grey rocks. At last, he saw something that looked a bit like his 'tooth', except that the pointy end was down instead of up.

'Is that it?' John asked the professor.

The professor pulled a big set of keys out of his pocket. He opened the glass lid of the case and took out the fossil, comparing it to John's specimen.

'What do you think?' he asked. 'I think they're similar.'

John agreed – they did look very similar.

'This is a fossil coral, actually. It's sometimes called a horn coral. Let's look at your other fossils,' the professor said.

John unwrapped them one by one. Together they managed to identify all of them. Professor

Baker admired John's trilobites and showed him even more in another cabinet. John's fossil centipede turned out to be the stalk of a fossilised sea lily or crinoid.

'It's a bit like a starfish that grows on a long, segmented stalk,' the professor explained. 'Trilobites and horn corals are **extinct**, but sea lilies still live in the ocean today.'

John marvelled at the huge jaws of gigantic marsupials. A large slab of rock was covered in delicate fish fossils that looked as if they were just about to swim away. Then the professor showed John a real dinosaur tooth. It was black and shiny with a brown root to it. The tooth was not sharp, but flat with little ridges on it.

'This is an *Iguanodon* tooth,' Professor Baker said, handing it to John. 'From southern England. This dinosaur lived in the Cretaceous Period, about 100 million years ago. See how the ridges on the side of the tooth would help it to grind down plants?'

John's eyes were wide with excitement. A real *Iguanodon* tooth! He was holding an actual dinosaur tooth from 100 million years ago. He handed it carefully to the professor, who put it back and locked the cabinet.

They all walked back to the reception area. Professor Baker shook their hands.

'You should keep up your studies, young man,' he said, as they left. 'You could become a **palaeontologist** one day – someone who studies fossils.'

John was quiet on the way home in the car. He couldn't believe that he had met a real scientist who studied fossils and rocks at university.

John learnt something very important that day – certain creatures only lived at certain prehistoric times. The oldest rocks had older forms of life in them, like trilobites and dinosaurs, and the more recent rocks had mammals and modern plants in them.

He didn't really understand what the professor had meant by geological time and evolution. But he understood that the age of the rocks told you what kinds of fossils to expect in different places.

If all the rocks at Lilydale were from the Devonian (400-360 million years ago), then there was no chance of ever finding dinosaurs there. Dinosaurs lived in the Mesozoic, about 250-65 million years ago. If he wanted to find dinosaurs, he'd have to look somewhere else.

> Rocks often form in layers with the oldest rocks at the bottom and the youngest ones on top. Sometimes these layers are upended but scientists can still tell how old they are by the fossils they find in them. Each of the layers have a name, like the Jurassic or the Devonian. This timeline in the rocks is called the **Geologic Time Scale.**

John's mind was spinning. It would take him a long time to make sense of all the things he'd heard that day.

Years later, John's mother told him that Professor Baker had written again, inviting John back to the University to meet the other lecturers and attend some classes on palaeontology. But John's mother thought that eight was much too young for him to go to university alone.

It didn't matter, though. John had realised two things for certain. Fossils were going to be the great passion of his life. And when he grew up, he was going to be a palaeontologist.

He couldn't wait to show his new collection to his cousin, Tim.

4

Underwater worlds

'Race you!' shouted Tim, as they ran out of the water and back up the beach. Tim was older than John, but John was faster. They laughed and shoved each other as they dashed across the sand and fell onto their towels, gasping for breath.

Summer with his cousins in Sandringham was John's favourite time of year. He could spend hours wandering along the cliffs and beaches of Black Rock, swimming or exploring the rock pools for crabs and shells.

When he was small, John's family had lived with the Flannerys in the same small house in Sandringham. Aunty Valda and John's mum were sisters. Tim was the oldest, a year and a half older than John, then Vicki, who was a year and a half younger and Penelope, who was three years younger.

Once, when John was about three and a half, he'd run away with his cousin, Vicki. Their mothers had been drinking tea and talking with friends, so John decided to take Vicki to the beach. They marched across busy Beach Road and through the sprawling tea tree scrub which grew on the foreshore.

'You won't believe it – I've just seen two scruffy little kids wandering *all by themselves* down Beach Road!' exclaimed one of his mum's friends as she arrived late.

'Where's John?' said his mum, dropping her teacup.

'Vicki!' Aunty Valda shouted.

They dashed outside, calling frantically for them, then raced across the road and down to the beach. They soon found John and Vicki playing happily in the sand with no idea what all the fuss was about.

Now, of course, John was nine and he and Tim were allowed to go to the beach by themselves whenever they liked.

'Look at this!' said Tim excitedly, showing John a stone he'd picked up. It was heart-shaped and about the size of one of the new 50-cent coins. John turned it over. One side was patterned with little holes in a five-armed star. On the other side was a big hole, like a mouth.

'I reckon it's a fossil,' John said. 'But I don't know what it is.'

John had already shown Tim his new fossil collection. They were both mad keen on dinosaurs and prehistoric animals.

'Mum says someone at the library might know about this stuff,' said Tim. 'Let's take it there this afternoon.'

After lunch, the boys walked around to the Sandringham Library where Tim was a regular visitor. They found the librarian re-shelving books and showed him their stone heart.

'It's looks like a fossil sea urchin, boys,' he said. 'You can find lots of them down at Beaumaris beach. But you should take it into the museum in the city and ask them.'

The boys looked at each other with excitement. The Beaumaris beach cliffs were only about five and a half kilometres down the coast. They couldn't wait to get there!

> **Beaumaris beach** is an internationally famous for its marine fossils including some very old fossils 430 million years old as well as more recent ones only 5 million years old. Many important sharks, whales, seabirds, shells and sea urchins have been found there.

The next day they headed down to Beaumaris. At the end of the beach, orange cliffs rose steeply out of the sand. Patches of scrub grew on the slopes. In other places the rocks had fallen down into the water. At the base of the cliffs they found heaps of fossilised sea urchins. Some of them even had pieces of sandy rock still clinging to them.

'It's the same rock as the cliffs up there,' said John, pointing up to a line in the rocks.

A whole bunch of fossilised sea urchins poked out of the orange sand, high up on the cliff, like ripe fruit ready to fall.

'So that's where they come from,' said Tim.

The clump of sea urchins was too high up to reach, but the boys soon found a few others buried in the lower layers of the cliff where they could dig them out with their pocketknives.

It was tiring work. After a while, John sat down on the sand for a rest and put his hand on something sharp. He picked it up. It was only small, not much bigger than a tic tac, with a sharp point and lots of serrations along the edge, like a steak knife.

'It's a tooth!' John shouted to Tim with excitement. 'I've found a tooth!'

Tim raced over to look.

'Definitely a tooth,' he agreed. 'We need to take that one into the museum.'

*

A few days later, they caught the train into the city to visit the Museum of Victoria on Swanston Street, in the same building as the State Library. The museum was filled with glass-topped cabinets of fossils from all over the world.

'Look, here are some fossils from Beaumaris,' John called to Tim. 'It says they're seven million years old!'

'Those are the sea urchins we found,' said Tim, pointing to some neat rows of heart-shaped disks. 'But look at these ones over here!'

The next cabinet held rows and rows of shark teeth from Beaumaris beach. Some were enormous – bigger than John's hand – the teeth of gigantic killer sharks, labelled as the prehistoric ancestors of the great whites.

'This reckons these sharks grew to 25 metres long,' read Tim, whistling. 'That's as big as a whale!'

'No way!' said John, his eyes wide. Who cared about dinosaurs when you could find a giant shark's tooth almost in your own backyard! Everyone knew there were lots of sharks in Port Phillip Bay. A great white shark had once taken a man who dived off the Middle Brighton pier. And that was only 16 kilometres from Beaumaris.

'Here's one like the tooth I found,' said John, comparing the sharp, little hooked tooth he'd found with others in the cabinet. 'It's from a tiger shark.'

Over the next few weeks, John and Tim spent most days fossil hunting at Beaumaris beach. At first, they waited for low tide to look for fossils in

the rock pools. When the tide was in, they hunted for bones or teeth in the cliffs. But the cliffs were soft and rocks often fell from above, so the boys soon decided that this was a bit too dangerous.

One day, they noticed a man standing waist-deep in the water with a bucket in front of him. Every now and again he'd dive his arm into the water and pull something out.

'What's he doing?' John wondered.

When the man came out of the water, the boys approached him.

'Did you find anything much?' they asked, gesturing to the bucket. It was always worth talking to other fossil collectors on the beach. The man showed them the empty bucket, which had a circle of glass stuck to the bottom. He put it in the water so they could see the bottom clearly.

The boys looked at each other.

'We've got to make ourselves one of them!' said Tim.

Their new friend turned out to be a local, Mr Colin Macrae, who'd been collecting fossils for years in the area. One day they visited Mr Macrae's house to see his vast collection. His wife made tea and offered cake, but even cake couldn't distract the boys from poring over the drawers full of bones and teeth.

'And this one,' Mr Macrae said holding up a small sliver of bone, 'is the rarest one of all! It's a fossil penguin. And it's going to be named after me.'

> This **fossil penguin** was described by the famous American palaeontologist Prof George Gaylord Simpson as *Pseudaptenodytes macraei* two years later in 1970. This species was probably twice the size of the fairy penguins that still breed on our beaches but nowhere near as big as the giant penguins, 150 cm tall, that once lived here.

*

John and Tim soon graduated from their home-made glass-bottomed bucket to snorkelling in the shallow waters. Algae and seaweed often hid the fossils underwater, but John quickly learnt to recognise shark's teeth by their shape. Over time, the boys became more adventurous, swimming out further and further where there were large stingrays and even small sharks.

They found sea urchins, shark teeth, seal jaws, whale ear bones, fish **vertebrae**, stingray stingers and giant penguin bones. They collected fossilised crabs, petrified barnacles and lots of different shells. Once, they even found a complete backbone from a large fossil whale.

After each trip, John soaked his specimens in diluted vinegar to dissolve the algae growing on them and then scrubbed them clean with an old toothbrush. Slimy green sharks' teeth soon gleamed as shiny as new. John could identify most of the sharks from their teeth and even which part of the jaw each tooth came from.

John's prized find was a giant mako shark tooth in perfect condition and nearly eight centimetres high. But the real goal was to find a huge tooth of a Megalodon, the giant distant relative of the great white sharks, whose tooth was as big as the palm of your hand. These ancient teeth were rare and often damaged.

There was always another bigger and better fossil to find on the next excursion. John's discoveries at Beaumaris beach with Tim would cement his passion for fossils for the rest of his life.

5

Meeting the big boss

John closed the book and added it to the pile on his desk. There were so many things he didn't understand about fossils. The books he borrowed from the library answered a lot of questions but still left him wondering.

How had dinosaurs grown so big with such small brains? How could one species have evolved from another? What caused an entire species to become extinct? Did a meteor wipe out the Cretaceous marine animals, like plesiosaurs and ammonites, along with the dinosaurs? Or was it something else? John tried to work the answers out for himself. He read over his notes and added his own thoughts.

John picked up the next book in the pile. He'd have to ask his parents to take him to the Camberwell Library again so they could borrow books from the adult section for him.

John was so engrossed in his project that he didn't notice Sister Martin watching him from across the classroom. She always let him work on his prehistoric projects if he finished his Maths or English work early. He was lucky to have a teacher who was as encouraging as Sister Martin.

When the bell rang to go home, Sister Martin walked over to him.

'I'd like you to come and talk to Father Keany, John,' she said. 'I've spoken to your parents. He'd like to hear about your projects too.'

Father Keany was the headmaster of Burke Hall at Xavier College. John didn't know why Father Keany wanted to talk to him, but he answered all the headmaster's questions as best he could. He brought out his notebooks and explained his ideas about the evolution of dinosaurs and about the different fossil shark teeth at Beaumaris. He wondered if he should have brought in some fossils, but Father Keany didn't seem to mind.

'So, how would you feel about going to Xavier College,' asked John's dad, later in the week.

John was surprised. Xavier College was a very expensive private school. His parents couldn't afford that.

'Father Keany has offered you a scholarship,' his mother explained. 'We'd still have to pay for the uniforms and sports gear and textbooks, but the fees would be less than usual.'

'You'd have to repeat Grade 5, though,' added his dad, 'so you're at the same level as the other boys.'

'I don't mind that,' said John, 'if you think it's a good idea. But can we afford it?'

'We don't mind putting in a few extra hours, John,' said his dad. 'I know you'll work hard, too, and make the most of it.'

John's dad was still working as a security attendant for the mining company, Rio Tinto. He checked each person who entered the building. Then he did the rounds after everyone left and locked up. John's mother also worked there now, delivering a trolley full of biscuits, tea and coffee to the executive offices.

John sometimes went there after school and sat drawing until his dad finished work. His dad introduced him to the geologists who worked in the building. They knew a lot about minerals, oil and gas, but some liked fossils, too.

One day, John's dad took him to the very top of the building which was ten floors higher than any other building in Melbourne.

'Sit on the edge,' said his dad, grinning, 'but hold on to the guard rail.'

John sat on the ledge and leaned on the rail, his legs swinging freely beneath. Far below – 99 metres to be exact – the people looked like ants streaming along the tiny footpaths. He could see all the way across the city to the Dandenong Ranges and out across the bay.

'The boss would like to meet you next week,' said his dad.

The director of Rio Tinto, Sir Maurice Mawby, had started collecting minerals when he was a boy in Broken Hill, but he was also very interested in plants and animals. When John's dad had told

Sir Maurice that John was compiling a book on Victorian fossils, he wanted to see it.

> **Broken Hill** is a famous mining town in the far west of NSW and the place where the big Australian mining company, BHP, started.

The big day came when John took the lift right up to the very top floor. He stepped into a room full of glass cabinets bristling with colourful mineral specimens. In the corner, John spied some fossils. They were from all over the world – Africa, America and Europe. Amongst them was a large green-blue shark's tooth with serrated edges, from Morocco.

Sir Maurice was very friendly, chatting happily as he looked through John's notebooks on Victorian fossils. Then he took John over to the fossil cabinet and pointed to some sharks' teeth.

'Any ideas what these ones might be?' he asked.

John had a closer look at the specimens. He was sure that some of them were great white sharks, possibly even megalodons, while others were extinct types of tiger sharks. He wrote the names down for Sir Maurice on a piece of paper.

'Thank you, John,' said Sir Maurice very politely. 'I appreciate your help.'

He waved his hand over the fossils.

'Perhaps you'd like to take one of these with you?'

John's eyes lit up. He really did fancy that beautiful blue-green shark's tooth. Without hesitation, Sir Maurice handed him the precious fossil and then shook his hand.

'Keep up the good work, young man,' he said. 'I look forward to hearing what you find in the future.'

'Thank you, sir,' replied John, feeling the cool smooth shark's tooth in his hand, his heart racing with excitement as he headed back out to the lift.

*

It was a long train ride home to Carrum, but John didn't mind. He spent his time drawing on the back of some old company share register forms his dad had given him. He finished drawing a picture of the horned dinosaur, *Ceratosaurus*, with an erupting volcano in the background. Then he looked at his last picture of marine life of the Cretaceous with nine different kinds of prehistoric marine reptiles, birds and invertebrates, and carefully labelled each

species with its name. By the time the train had sped past Sandringham, where he collected so many fossils with Tim, John had started on a new drawing.

'What sort of fish is that?' asked his dad, reading out the name, Coelacanth. 'A Ko-ell-a-kanth?'

'It's pronounced seel-uh-kanth' said John. 'I read about in the *National Geographic*. It was discovered in 1938 by a museum curator in South Africa. She noticed this beautiful silver-and-blue fish on a fishing boat. She'd never seen any fish like it before, so she took it back to the museum in a taxi.'

'Bet the taxi driver didn't like that,' commented John's dad. 'How big is it?'

'About a metre,' John replied. 'Her boss told her to throw it away. Said it was just a common rock cod.'

'It doesn't look much like rock cod to me,' said John's dad, looking at the thick fleshy fins and a three-lobed tail that John had drawn.

'It's got a thick scaly armour too, and a strange head and jaw,' said John.

'Think I might prefer a nice whiting for dinner, myself,' said his dad, going back to his newspaper.

As John coloured in the Coelacanth on his page, he thought about how amazing the discovery of this '**living fossil**' had been. It was like a window into the past and gave clues about how ancient fish had moved onto the land. It was incredible to think that a fish like this had developed legs and lungs and gradually evolved into reptiles, mammals, even people.

There was still much for John to discover.

> The rediscovery of the **Coelacanth** caused a sensation. This fish was thought to have become extinct 65 million years ago. Twenty thousand people came to the museum to look at the first one found and a reward was offered to anyone catching another one. It took 14 years before another one was found and there was an international battle over who owned the dead fish.

6

A new school

John tapped the shaly rock, splitting it apart. Inside were the characteristic fronds of a graptolite – like black seaweed drawn onto the grey stone. John and his friend Simon often came over to Studley Park to look for graptolites after school – when they weren't playing cricket or football. John brushed the dust off his grey school uniform and pushed his cap into his bag along with his discarded school tie.

'Simon!' he called. 'Found a good one!'

Simon was busy looking down the edge of the slope towards the Yarra River. He waved for John to come closer. Something was wrong.

> **Graptolites** are rare but important fossils for calculating the age of rocks. Although they occurred all over the world for a very long time, it is easy to tell the age of the rock by the different types of graptolites found.

Simon pointed to a pile of corrugated iron on the slope. John looked closer. There was an arm sticking out from underneath.

The boys slid down to take a closer look. Carefully lifting the sheet of iron with a stick, they saw a scruffy old man lying there with his mouth open and head lolled back.

'He's dead!' whispered Simon.

'Quick,' said John, 'we'd better tell someone.'

The boys ran back to school and found a teacher still in the yard.

'There's a dead body by the river!' they shouted.

The teacher called the police, who listened carefully to the boys' story.

'You better show us where it is,' the policeman said.

Back at the river the boys pointed to their grim discovery. The policeman slid down the slope and lifted the sheet of iron. He put his hand out and gently shook the man's arm.

John jumped as the body groaned and moved. The policeman gave him another shake and the old man slowly opened his eyes and began swearing loudly at them for disturbing his sleep!

'Nothing to worry about here, lads,' said the policeman grinning. 'Best be on your way.'

That wasn't the discovery John had been expecting when he went to the park after school that day!

*

John enjoyed his new school and making new friends. They played ball in the playground at lunchtime or, if it was too wet, table tennis in the hall. In winter he had to play full forward in Aussie Rules football on Saturday mornings, which was better than the boring cricket matches in summer. As soon as he could, though, he swapped to soccer in winter and swimming in summer.

The school also had an excellent library where John spent a lot of time reading and where he soon discovered *The Hobbit* and *Lord of the Rings*.

John's family had moved house to Carrum, a two-hour commute every day to school. In winter, it was often dark when John left home and dark by the time he got back, which didn't leave much time for anything else. Their house was only a short walk from the beach and the mouth of the Patterson River – a great place for catching bream on the weekend.

But it was still the fossil trips that excited John the most. John and Tim would often take plastic ice-cream tubs of fossils into the museum in the city for identification.

'Hmm ... now this one is interesting,' the curator of palaeontology, Dr Tom Darragh, would often say. 'I think we'll have to go downstairs and check in the collection.'

John and Tim loved going down into the museum 'dungeons' behind the bright, airy public display areas. 'Back of house' was a maze of dark corridors. The cabinets and shelves were stacked with stuffed animals, skeletons, jars of pickled fish and even dried heads. Dug-out canoes hung from the ceiling.

'Ah, here we are,' said the curator, pulling out a drawer of fossils similar to the ones the boys had found. The museum was full of treasures. John thought Dr Darragh was really lucky to work there. He could spend a lifetime exploring these collections and never get bored.

One of the geology students they met at the museum invited John on a field trip to Waurn Ponds quarry near Geelong, to look for fossilised sharks' teeth. This site was much older than Beaumaris so there were many different kinds of teeth to add to John's collection.

John had been gradually learning all the names of the shark species as well as how to tell an upper tooth from a lower tooth and a tooth from the front of the jaw from a tooth at the back. So when he found a beautifully preserved serrated shark's tooth at the quarry site he knew exactly what it was.

'It's an upper second anterior from *Carcharodon auriculatus* – a close relative of the megalodon,' John announced at dinner, holding up the prized tooth.

'Really?' replied his dad. 'It's a beauty, alright!'

His dad put his fork down.

'How about a trip to Minhamite next week? Up near Hamilton? I've found a farmhouse we can stay in.'

John's family often organised fossil hunting trips away for both the boys. The area around Hamilton in the Western District of Victoria was a favourite.

A local fossil collector showed them all the best places to collect. The creeks that ran through the town had cut away cliffs of blue clay, white limestone and a gritty mudstone, all with their own distinct types of marine fossils from different ages. In the soft clay on top of the marine layers, they found 150,000-year-old blackened bones of giant prehistoric marsupials.

They would walk for hours across paddocks and creeks, climbing through barbed-wire fences and dodging angry bulls as they went. In summer, when the water was low, they walked around the lakes in the Western District, searching for the jawbones of giant Tasmanian devils or the footprints of **diprotodons.**

Fossils weren't the only great finds, though. One night they went fishing in the river. Instead of the silver perch or blackfish they expected to hook, John caught a gigantic freshwater eel. Unlike the other fish, it didn't thrash about helplessly gasping for air. Instead, it lifted up its head, looked around and bolted for the nearest shallow pothole in the river. The boys dashed into the mud after it, wrestling the slippery creature into an icebox.

They sat on the lid as the eel thumped inside.

'Do you think we should eat it?' asked Tim.

'How're we going to kill it?' said John.

The lid of the icebox jumped. The eel certainly wasn't about to give up easily.

'Reckon we've caught enough fish for a meal, anyway,' said Tim.

'Yeah. How about we let this one go,' agreed John.

So they carried the icebox down to the bank, tipped it over and cracked open the lid.

In a flash, the eel slipped out across the grass and disappeared into the water. John couldn't help wondering how a fish could breathe on land as well as it could underwater.

*

'What do you think of this?' said Tim one weekend, showing John an entry form he'd picked up in the museum. 'It's for the Science Talent Search. Should we go in it?'

John read the piece of paper out loud.

'Girls and boys of outstanding ability in science can receive bursaries in the 1970 Science Talent

Search. For full-time students at Victorian schools and colleges under 18 and over 13 years of age.'

'Sounds pretty cool – what's a bursary?' asked John, handing the flyer back.

'Prize money. The winner gets $70. We'd have to enter the Intermediate Division since I'm in Form 3,' said Tim, who was in year 9, a couple of years ahead of John at school. 'But we could do something on the recent fossils of Victoria. We've got plenty of material for that.'

John had just started high school. He loved Art and English, but he also liked Latin, French and Ancient Greek because they helped him understand scientific names which often used a hybrid of Latin and Greek words. But there was nothing in his Science lessons about biology or geology. He struggled through Maths, Physics and Chemistry, which didn't interest him much. This project was the kind of science he liked.

For the next few weeks, the boys spent all their spare time filling a notebook with descriptions of their best specimens. And to their huge surprise, they won a runner-up prize in the competition!

The next year, John decided to enter on his own in the Junior Division. His entry was: 'A study of the various fossil remains found in Victoria'.

One morning at school assembly, when John was not really paying attention, he heard his name mentioned.

'And we are delighted to announce that John Long has won…first prize in the Victorian Science Talent Quest,' declared the principal.

There was a polite round of applause, mostly from the Science teacher, Mr Darcy.

'Well done, John,' said the principal, before quickly moving on to the weekend football results.

The prize was $60, sponsored by Western Mining Corporation. Better still, John had to display his winning project in the museum in the city and talk to the public about his work.

John proudly set up his specimens in the two wooden glass-topped display cases that his dad had made for him. When the hall opened to the public, people crowded in, jostling to see the specimens and read all the labels. John loved chatting to everyone – from excited children to old ladies; people who knew a lot about fossils and many who didn't.

He couldn't imagine anything he'd like to do more than work in a museum and talk to people about fossils every day!

> The **Science Talent Search** is still run in Victoria with similar competitions in other states. There are lots of competitions for school students across a wide range of different sciences.

7

Camping chaos

John woke up early one Christmas morning and headed quietly into the lounge room. He looked under the tree in the corner where a small pile of presents was to see if the large rectangular shape he'd been hoping for was among them.

He picked up the heavy package and sat down on the lounge to unwrap it. The size and weight was right. He'd held a book this size many times in the library and longed to have his own copy.

John slid the hard book out of the paper. There it was, with the stegosaurus emblazoned on the cover. His very own copy of Josef Augusta's *Prehistoric Animals*. He opened the pages and started to carefully leaf through it. There were 60 pages of images, mostly black and white but some in full colour, by the renowned artist Zdenek Burian. He noticed the price, $5.25, pencilled on the front page and whistled quietly. That was a lot of money for his parents.

John was reading his book from one end to the other when his parents got up. John's dad sat next to him, wincing a bit as he lowered himself down slowly. He'd always had a bit of a bad back.

'Good book, John?' he asked.

John grinned and gave his dad a hug.

'Thanks, Dad. Thanks, Mum,' he said, happily. 'It's just what I wanted.'

His mum smiled.

'I'm sure it will get plenty of use,' she said. 'Now, come and have some breakfast. You can bring the book with you, if you like.'

*

One afternoon, John got home late from school. The house was unusually quiet and he couldn't smell dinner cooking either. John was always starving after school so dinner was usually on the table as soon as he came in.

'I'm home,' he called, dropping his bag in the hallway. He found his mum sitting at the kitchen table.

'Oh, John,' she said standing up, 'I'd better get you some dinner.'

'What's wrong?' he asked. It wasn't like his mum not to have dinner ready. 'Where's Dad?'

'Your dad's at the hospital,' she replied. 'He collapsed at work today. Something's wrong with his back. He's having some tests.'

'Will he be okay?' asked John.

'I don't know,' his mum replied. 'They think his spine was damaged from an injury in the war and now it's wearing out. He might end up in a wheelchair.'

John's dad had to retire early from his work. His back injury meant that he couldn't keep working at Rio Tinto, but at least he wasn't in a wheelchair. His pension wasn't enough for them to live on.

'What are we going to do, Mum?' asked John.

'It's going to be hard,' she replied, shaking her head. 'We're thinking of running a milk bar close to your school. Your dad can help out when he's well and we'll need your help after school.'

They moved into the tiny flat above the milk bar in Kew and made it as homely as they could. Each morning, John would get up before sunrise, bring in the milk, bread, newspaper and magazine deliveries and get the shop ready to open. Then he'd serve in the shop while his parents sorted the orders for the day or paid for incoming goods.

John was used to getting up early, anyway, and he preferred helping his mum and dad in the shop rather than travelling for so many hours every day to school. At about 8.30 a.m., he headed off to school which was only a few minutes' walk away. After school he helped with cleaning, serving or sorting supplies. He knew how hard his parents had to work to support his education, so he'd do anything he could do to help them.

John's parents still did their best to support his interest in fossils. One day his dad came home with some scientific books by the Bureau of Mineral Resources from a relative who worked for the Government Printing Office. John found them very technical, but he loved one series on palaeontology. They were full of pictures of jaws and teeth and fossil bones. One of them included the first detailed description of a small, armoured fish, known as a placoderm, from the Northern Territory.

> **Placoderms** are extinct armoured fishes that lived in the oceans from 440-380 million years ago. They were the first fish to have jaws with teeth. Placoderm means plate-skinned in Greek.

This particular fish, *Bothriolepis*, with its armour of interlocking plates, intrigued John. It looked like a cross between a crab and a tortoise with a curved dome of a body and two long leg-like fins on each side. Like other placoderms – it was covered in bony armour pitted with a network of tiny dots for which it was named. *Bothriolepis* was Greek for pitted scale.

He copied the drawing into his notebooks as part of his submission for the Science Talent Search.

John's entry on 'A brief history of Victoria's Fishes and Sharks' was 104 pages long with over 100 illustrations, an index and references. It had many previously undescribed fossil fish bones which, even today, have still never been published.

But, despite all his work, John only won a minor $10 prize. He was a bit disappointed.

'You can't win every year, John,' said his mother. 'They have to let others have a turn.'

The mysterious little *Bothriolepis* continued to puzzle him, though. If there were *Bothriolepis* fish in the Northern Territory, maybe there were some in Victoria, too?

John was determined that one day, he'd find them.

*

John pulled his backpack out of the car boot and onto the busy footpath near the railway station on Spencer Street in the city.

'Simon, can you give us a hand with the tent?' he called.

Simon was checking that the luggage was all secure while John's parents helped unload the rest of their equipment.

'You sure you've got everything you need, boys?' asked John's dad.

'Yep,' John replied, 'it's all sorted.'

They'd been planning this trip for weeks. This was their first real expedition with no adult supervision. They'd organised it all themselves, hiring equipment and booking travel. It was going to be John's fifteenth birthday while they were away and he couldn't think of a better way to celebrate.

A shout from down the street made John look up. Tim and his friend Brian came towards them loaded up with their gear.

The boys piled onto the train for the five-hour trip to Hamilton. By mid-afternoon they found themselves standing alone on the quiet country train platform with only a few chirping sparrows for company. They wandered down to the local shop to buy some food for the week then headed for their campsite.

'How far is it?' Tim asked.

'Not too far,' John said, looking at their map. 'It's just down the road a bit.'

It didn't take long before the boys realised it was hard work lugging all their gear along a country road. They were very relieved to see the approaching dust cloud of a farm ute coming towards them.

'Need a lift, boys?' asked the farmer, grinning. 'Been expecting you.'

Mr George Pelchen owned the land where the fossil sites were and had agreed to let the boys come and stay for a few days. George was a keen fossil fossicker himself and told them all about the fossil treasures he'd picked up over many years of farming in this part of Victoria. The boys hoped they'd have just as much luck.

'Yeah, as long as you get something, that's the main thing,' said old George Pelchen, something he often repeated, much to the boys' amusement.

By the time George dropped the boys off at their campsite it was getting late. They quickly set up the tents and got the campsite ready. It was thirsty work, so John went to collect some water from the creek and made up some orange cordial, handing the cups to Tim and Brian who gulped the sweet liquid down.

'Did you boil that water?' asked Simon.

'Nuh,' said John, pouring himself another cup. 'Can't beat fresh water from the creek!'

They heated up some tinned stew on a small stove for dinner and wolfed it down. Afterwards,

Tim rummaged in his bag, bringing out a big bag of Brazil nuts.

'Dessert,' he declared.

Feeling very sophisticated, the boys cracked Brazil nuts, played cards and drank cups of weak instant coffee that Simon made.

Their expedition was off to a flying start. Tired after their long day, they all crawled into the tent and into their sleeping bags, looking forward to finding lots of fossils the next day.

In the night, John woke with a strange sensation in his stomach. He sat up, wondering what was wrong. The grumble turned into a rumble and then a roar. He dashed for the opening of the tent. But it was too late. A potent brew of orange cordial, stew and chunks of Brazil nuts erupted through his nose and mouth. Violent convulsions wracked his body as he emptied his stomach of all its contents.

He could hardly move from the entrance of the tent when, suddenly, Tim clambered over him, cursing as he slipped in the pile of vomit outside. Brian soon followed and from the sounds of chundering coming out of the bushes they were both suffering just as much as John.

All through the night, the three boys were violently ill and the smell in and around the tent got worse and worse.

Morning dawned on a horrible sight. Simon, who had slept soundly, woke to find himself surrounded by groaning bodies, covered in vomit and who knew what else.

'Please, get help.'

'I just want to die.'

'Make it stop.'

Simon went to get some more water from the creek and boiled it carefully before making them all some weak sweet tea to sip on. He offered them some dry biscuits but the thought of eating still made them feel sick. He cleaned up as best he could before heading into town for help. At least it got him away from the smell!

Brian and Tim lay in the tent, glaring at John whenever they had the strength to do so.

'The cordial from hell, hey, John?' muttered Brian. 'Good one!'

'I'm never drinking orange cordial again,' groaned Tim.

'Well, I'm NEVER drinking water again,' said John bitterly. 'Just in case.'

Simon returned from the long walk to town with some medicine to ease the nausea, but it still took a couple of days for them to recover.

On the third day, Simon wandered back from the creek with a handful of sharks' teeth to show them.

'I reckon I can make it down there if we go slowly,' Brian said, perking up a bit.

'Come on,' said John. 'Let's go.'

The fossils worked their magic. Before long all four boys were busy collecting bits of whale bone, oyster shells and other marine creatures from five million years ago. By the evening they were ravenously hungry, but this time they made sure to boil their drinking water! That night they all slept soundly.

From that disastrous start, the trip could only get better. They walked along the creek line, several kilometres south of Grange Burn to Muddy Creek. The exposed blue clays of Muddy Creek were famous for their gigantic cowrie and volute shells. It was amazing to think that the sea had once covered large parts of inland Australia.

As they wandered along the creek, Tim suddenly stopped and plunged his hands into the cold

running water. He held up a huge perfect tooth, bigger than anything John had ever seen before.

It was as big as his hand – a perfect triangle, with finely serrated edges. There was no mistaking it.

'It's a Megalodon,' said John. 'The giant killer shark.'

'How did you spot that?' exclaimed Brian looking at the beautiful tooth as it glinted in the light.

Tim just shrugged.

'I just saw it lying there,' he replied.

That was just so like Tim, John thought. He had such a great knack for spotting rare things that others walked past.

On their last night, Mr Pelchen invited them to the farmhouse for dinner. As they walked up to the house at twilight, they could smell a heavenly roast dinner drifting on the air towards them. While they all tucked in, Mr Pelchen regaled them with stories of the district's history while the boys told them about their discoveries.

'And then there was the cordial,' muttered Brian.

John recounted their misadventure with the creek water.

'Oh, no,' cried Mrs Pelchen, 'you can't drink from the creek!'

Mr Pelchen shook his head.

'All the town sewage runs into that creek,' he said. 'Probably got the worst bugs in the world!'

'Lucky you've got strong constitutions, boys,' said Mrs Pelchen as she brought out still more food to ladle onto their plates.

Just when John thought he couldn't fit anything more in, Mrs Pelchen brought out a special treat. Someone started singing 'Happy Birthday' and Mrs Pelchen put a big cake in front of him.

'Happy fifteenth birthday, John,' she said.

'This is amazing!' John declared as the cheers faded. 'I think this is probably the best birthday I've ever had.'

'Even with the cordial from hell?' added Brian.

'Well, as long as you got something,' said Mr Pelchen, absent-mindedly, sending them all off into peals of laughter.

8

Karate kid

The doors of the cinema sprang open and the boys ran down the steps talking excitedly.

'That was amazing!' John exclaimed.

'Those moves!' said John's schoolmate, Michael. 'Bruce Lee's been doing kung fu since he was 13.'

'It'd be great to be able to fight like that,' said John, mimicking some of the kicks he'd seen in the movie.

'And he's not even very tall' Michael said, who had been learning karate for a couple of years.

'Doesn't matter what size you are. Why don't you come with me to training on Saturday?'

That weekend John arrived at the Bob Jones School of Zen-Do Kai, down the bottom of Elizabeth Street in the city, to watch both boys and girls training in karate. They looked like modern-day warriors, in flowing black robes or crisp white uniforms as they worked their way through kicks, blocks and pre-arranged fighting routines.

It all looked very disciplined and controlled, just like the movies, rather than a free-for-all like other sports. John felt as if he got flattened just about every weekend at football or soccer. Karate looked like great fun and no one seemed to get hurt. This sport was about learning to protect yourself from injuries, not running straight into them.

'What do you think?' asked Michael, flopping down in the seat beside John.

'Yeah – I'll give it a go,'

After that, John started training regularly. He loved the discipline and precision of the movement and the way he improved with every class. The only time he got hurt was when he'd done something wrong. Best of all, it gave him the confidence to tackle larger opponents, even if he lost. Even then he felt that he'd learnt something valuable.

John soon earned a junior blue belt with a white stripe. He loved the idea that with regular training you could advance up the ranks, one belt at a time. He wasn't just running around an oval every weekend, doing exactly the same thing. Instead, he was always improving, even as his task got harder.

'If a belt is your goal, you'll quit when you receive it,' one of the trainers told him. 'If knowledge is your goal, you'll never stop training.'

John really liked that idea. From then on, he went to see every Bruce Lee movie ever made many times over, saving up enough pocket money to see *Way of the Dragon* seven times at the cinema. He even convinced the school sportsmaster to let him do karate instead of the compulsory school sports.

For a while, everything John did was about karate.

*

'Well done, John, you've won the subject prize for English this year,' said the English teacher. 'Any idea what kind of book you'd like for your prize?'

'A book on karate, please, sir.'

The English teacher looked a little startled but, at the end of the year, John was given George Mattson's *The Way of Karate*.

He couldn't wait to read it but to his surprise, he found that this version of karate was completely different from the one he was learning. So, he showed the book to one of the teachers, or Sensei, at the school.

'This is a traditional style of karate from the island of Okinawa,' the Sensei said. 'These old Okinawan masters were renowned for their feats of skill and strength. It's a good book. You will learn a lot from it.'

'But not how to beat me,' joked one of the older boys. 'That stuff's no good for street fighting. That's what you learn here!'

'The karate at this school does include street defence,' agreed the Sensei.

'There's plenty of work for black belts in security,' the other boy added. 'Once I've got my green belt, I'm going to the Sunbury Rock Festival as a security guard.'

John didn't want to work as a security guard, even at a rock festival, but he did want to get his green belt.

*

John bowed deeply and stood tall with his feet together. He held his arms straight with his hands overlapping in front of him. Then he jumped, landing with feet spread and arms crossed out in front. He breathed in loudly and brought his arms down on either side, fists clenched and stomach tensed. Strike left, pull back, across. Twist. Strike right, pull back, across. Twist.

The Sanchin kata or 'ironbody' sequence was gruelling. It required intense focus on every muscle in the body and was designed to ensure that students had strengthened all their core muscles into a strong body armour. But if the training was gruelling, it was nothing compared to the testing.

John kept his expression impassive as he faced one of the most senior sensei in the dojo. Richard Norton was a second-degree black belt, who would go on to become a famous Hollywood martial arts actor and stuntman.

Right now, Richard was looking at John with a fierce glare intended to terrify his opponent. John kept his face as stony as he hoped his muscles were. Richard was about to put all John's training to the test.

In a flash, Richard struck John hard in the stomach. John hissed through gritted teeth but did not move. Repeatedly Richard struck John on the arms, legs and stomach, making sure that every muscle was tensed and unmoving like a body of iron. Finally, Richard grunted and moved on to the next candidate. John relaxed his pose slightly, but it wasn't over yet. One by one the more experienced provisional green belts, stepped in front to see if they could beat John into defeat.

The sparring seemed to go on forever – a flurry of strikes, sweeps and kicks: back thrust, tornado, front snap, jumping double and axe. But John stood firm and remained standing as others fell to their knees around him. Finally, the last green belt stepped away. John had passed! He was a green belt, 5th kyu, and halfway to reaching his goal of being a black belt or 1st dan.

Every now and again big sparring competitions were held at the Melbourne Town Hall. Everyone poured out of the dojo, down the stairs onto Elizabeth Street, running down the street, excited and exuberant, in their flowing white karate uniforms, the sensei standing out in black. Around the corner along Collins Street, they streamed through the grand archways of the Town Hall.

As a green belt, John was allowed to watch the secretive black belt gradings. These involved almost superhuman feats of endurance. John watched as they did a hundred knuckle push-ups and a hundred sit-ups without even pausing. Then two gruelling hours of karate techniques and self-defence. Finally, there was a brutal sparring session, with ten other brown and black belts pushing the new candidates to their limits.

Finally, the successful candidates stepped up to receive their black belts. Everyone clapped loudly in genuine admiration. It was such an achievement. In John's eyes they were all true Bushido warriors. He was determined that he would never give up karate and that one day he would make black belt level too.

In the meantime, as a green belt with a brown stripe, John had to compete with adults even though he was a fairly small 17-year-old. The sparring was pretty tough. In one match, he was knocked unconscious when a tall black belt swept John's legs out from underneath him and his head cracked on the wooden floor.

When John began his final year at school, he decided that he couldn't afford to keep getting injured, so he took up Wu Tai Chi – a much gentler style of martial arts. John enjoyed the three hours' training in the park, improving his strength and health. And it was here that he developed a new interest.

One day after Wu Tai Chi, John overheard some of the men talking about a motorbike for sale.

'It's a 175 two-stroke Honda,' he was told. 'With a pressed-steel frame. Only two hundred dollars, if you're interested.'

John had ridden Tim's old 250 Jawa Californian a few times and he was really keen to have his own. He'd already done the simple written exam for his learner's permit, so all he needed was a bike to ride and L plates. Convincing his parents this was a good idea was harder.

'Tim's been riding his for a couple of years now and he's fine,' John argued. 'I won't have to wait around for trains to get home.'

And so, one rainy winter's day John went to pick up the first of many motorcycles. It was a long way to the factory in Moorabbin and the train drivers were on strike, so he had to wait for a bus.

By the time he picked up the red Honda, it was peak hour and starting to get dark. The roads were busier because of the train strike and it was raining heavily – not good conditions to be riding a motorbike, anyway, but the worst possible conditions for a brand-new learner rider who kept stalling his bike in the middle of the Nepean Highway.

By the time he got home, John was wondering whether the bike was a horrible mistake. But he quickly got the hang of it and loved taking off to go wherever he liked. He even rode it to school and parked around the corner so he didn't get into trouble with the teachers.

*

When the exam results came out at the end of his final year of school, John had done well enough to get into the University of Melbourne. But then his parents revealed that they also had plans.

'We're moving to the Gold Coast in Queensland,' his mother announced one evening.

'Why?' asked John.

'The weather will be better for your dad. Land's cheap and we can build a nice house there,' she explained.

'That'll cost a fortune,' John said.

'Not if we do it ourselves,' his dad replied. 'You could come and give us a hand in the holidays.'

'I've got a better idea,' said John. 'I'll take a gap year and help you build the house first. University can wait.'

*

'If you're going up to the Gold Coast,' Tim said, 'why not just keep going?'

'Where to?' asked John.

'Up to Cairns. And then to Cooktown. We could ride the bikes.'

Tim was at university already, studying literature at La Trobe University. But he was still just as keen as John about fossils – and motorbikes and adventures.

'Brian's up for it,' Tim added. 'What do you reckon? We could head up there by March and still get back in time for you to start work on the house.'

'That'd give me a few months to work here and save up for the trip,' John said, starting to get excited.

'Great,' Tim said, 'but just don't bring any of that cordial, hey?'

John grinned. He'd never live down that cordial story. But a trip up to **Cooktown** sounded like a great idea. He looked at a map. He'd be halfway there already from the Gold Coast. They'd done heaps of trips before all over Victoria, but he'd never gone interstate before. He didn't think it would take long to get up north and into some real wilderness.

> Check out where **Cooktown** is and find out how many kilometres they travelled to get there from Melbourne.

*

It felt as if they'd been riding for days before they had even crossed the Queensland border from New South Wales. When they looked at the map, they couldn't believe that they were only halfway to their destination.

'Australia really is a pretty big country, hey?' John said to Tim.

John had saved up just enough money for the trip, working in a hotel opposite the Melbourne Cricket Ground. Even so, he had to be pretty careful to make his money last. They bought cheap bags of tropical fruit from roadside stalls and stuffed themselves with bananas or pineapples. At night, they camped in the bush next to their bikes, in sleeping bags on the ground. It certainly wasn't luxurious.

By the time they got up north it was March — and still the wet season.

'And everyone reckons that Melbourne's wet,' shouted Tim over the sound of the rain pummelling on the verandah as they stopped in a small country town up north. Water flowed over the edge like a waterfall and flooded the roadway.

'How long before this rain eases up?' John asked a local leaning against a verandah post.

'About May,' the man replied.

'What!' shouted John. 'It can't last that long. How do you get anything done?'

The local shrugged and finished his can of drink. 'Might ease up on Monday, mate. Bit o' rain never hurt.'

He tossed his can in the bin and stepped out into the deluge, his thongs slapping through the water.

John looked at the others.

'Looks like we're just going to have to get wet,' he remarked.

Rain wasn't the worst of it. Rivers flooded the roadways everywhere; often there didn't seem to be any way around them. They pushed their bikes through the muddy waters swirling with debris, all the while keeping their eyes peeled for crocodiles. Once they reached the other side, they had to strip the bikes down to make sure there was no water in the air filters or cylinders.

Eventually, they reached the Mossman River on the southern edge of the Daintree rainforest. There was no pushing the bikes across this river – apart from the crocs, it was too wide and deep. Luckily, they found a narrow sugarcane train track that crossed the river on a bridge especially built for it. The train driver agreed to carry them and their bikes across in one of the cane bins, that looked like a toy goods train carriage. From here they followed muddy roads that were more like bush tracks, with thick rainforest on one side and white reef-fringed beaches on the other.

By the time they reached Cooktown, everything was soaked. John's sleeping bag was mouldy and didn't smell too good so he threw it in the bin.

'What are you going to sleep in now when you get back south?' asked the others.

'I've got my motorbike leathers,' he replied.

John remembered a friend telling him that, 'Any fool can be uncomfortable camping'. Next time, he thought, he'd make sure he was better prepared.

9

You'll never get a job

The waves pounded along the beach near Inverloch, southeast of Melbourne. It was cold and windy and the sea was rough. John and Tim pushed into the wind as they followed Rob Glenie towards a large rocky headland. Rob was a geologist they'd met at the museum and they were helping him with some fieldwork.

'There it is,' said Rob, pointing. 'Eagles Nest.'

At the end of the headland, the rocks rose from the water like a ruined castle. Flat rocks stretched around the base. Now and again a large wave surged across the surface and hissed angrily as it retreated

'We should start on the other side and work our way back,' said Rob. 'We've got an hour before the tide's too high.'

He pulled a map from his backpack and opened it as the wind tried to tug it out of his hands. It was an old, hand-drawn map with the different types of rocks coloured in blue, green, yellow and brown. Neatly printed text labelled the coast with notes.

John pointed to a spot marked A, on an outcrop of Jurassic sandstone.

'A few fragments of bone and **coprolites** of reptiles found here,' he read.

'What are our chances?' asked Tim, 'It's been 75 years and plenty of people have looked before.'

A large wave crashed across the headland with a boom.

Coprolite is another name for fossilised faeces. *Tyrannosaurus rex* coprolites can weigh over 9 kg. Coprolites tell scientists a lot about the food prehistoric animals ate, how their digestive systems worked and what their environment was like.

'It's a new site after every high tide,' John pointed out. 'Something could be uncovered today and gone tomorrow. We might be lucky.'

'Let's go, then!' Rob yelled into the wind.

They headed across the slippery rocks, keeping one eye on the sea and the other on the unstable cliffs.

'This is the spot!' Rob shouted to the others. 'This is where he found it.'

Ever since he'd found his first fossil in the quarry at Lilydale, John had dreamt of finding a dinosaur fossil. But dinosaur bones were very rare in Australia. Fragments of dinosaurs had turned up over the years – mostly in Queensland. A few came from the opal fields, but nothing like the great skeletons found in America and Europe.

Only one dinosaur fragment had ever been found in Victoria. It was a tiny toe bone found by a geologist on the very spot where John now stood. It was his map that they were using. But that was 75 years ago and nothing more had been found since.

It wasn't easy to look for fossils here. You couldn't just dig into the rock and hope to find something. That would be like searching for a needle in a very large, rock-hard, haystack. To find good sites, you had to search areas exposed by rivers, mining, roadworks or tunnels.

One hundred million years ago, the coast at Inverloch had been a wide river valley between Australia and Antarctica. Antarctica had split away and now the sea was exposing the rocks from the river valleys where dinosaurs might once have walked. At least at low tide and in good weather, anyway.

> The **Inverloch fossil site** is the richest early Cretaceous dinosaur fossil site in Australia and is of international significance. It contains small dinosaur remains from a time when southern Australia was close to the South Pole.

John scanned the rock shelf for fossil-like shapes. It was hard to see anything in the wet reflective surfaces. He peered into a rock pool and noticed an unusual looking pebble. It was probably nothing.

He picked it up anyway. It had a strange mesh-like pattern. This wasn't geological; this was organic. It was bone.

'Hey,' he shouted over the wind to the others and waving his hand. 'Found something!'

The others hurried over.

'What is it?' asked Tim.

John held out the pebble for them to look at.

'Well, I reckon it's from a dinosaur,' he said.

*

Back at the museum in Melbourne they showed John's find to the new curator of palaeontology Tom Rich. Tom and his wife, Pat Vickers-Rich, were young and enthusiastic palaeontologists who had arrived from America a few years earlier. Pat was a lecturer at Monash University.

'Unbelievable!' exclaimed Tom. 'And this was the first thing you picked up?'

He passed the fossil fragment to Pat.

'It's definitely dinosaur,' she confirmed.

'The first fossil is the hardest one to find,' Tom said, looking pleased. 'After that, you know where to keep looking.'

Tom and Pat were interested in the vertebrate fossils of mammals, reptiles, birds and fish – not just invertebrates like insects and molluscs. John and Tim had volunteered on many of their digs.

> **Vertebrates** are animals with backbones and internal skeletons, like fish, mammals and reptiles. **Invertebrates** don't have a backbone but often have their 'bones' on the outside, like an exoskeleton. Insects, worms, shells and jellyfish are all invertebrates.

'How are your studies going, John?' asked Pat.

John was in his second year of studying science at Melbourne University. He now went to lectures in the very same Old Geology Building that he had visited with his dad all those years ago as a kid.

Professor Baker had retired and Professor Owen Singleton was now the professor in the Geology Department. He didn't think much of John's interest in vertebrate palaeontology. John thought he was like a grumpy walrus.

'You'll never get a job in vertebrate palaeontology,' Professor Singleton had said sternly. 'Study geology. There's plenty of work in mining.'

It wasn't a good start. At least John could finally study biology and palaeontology, but it was mostly about invertebrates and not much on vertebrates.

John looked at Pat and Tom. They had found jobs as palaeontologists. Maybe he could find palaeontology work in America one day?

'I've done nearly all of the zoology, botany and geology subjects I can now – as well as all four palaeontology courses,' said John, replying to Pat's question. 'I've run out of things I want to study.'

'You need to transfer to Monash,' she said. 'You'll get credit for all the subjects you've already done and you can do third year with us – in vertebrate palaeontology.'

'It's a good plan, John,' said Tom. 'If you want to work in palaeontology, you'll need to do an honours project, then a **doctorate**. Pat is the best person in Victoria to supervise that if you want to do a PhD on vertebrates. Actually, she's the only person.'

> Scientists learn how to do research by studying at university. Usually, they do a first or undergraduate degree which takes about 4 years. Then they often do a very large research project called a **doctorate** or **PhD**, which takes more than three years to finish.

As John and Tim walked back to the train station to go home, John thought about Pat and Tom's suggestion.

'It would be a big move,' said John.

'You should swap,' said Tim. 'There's no point being at Melbourne Uni if you can't study the things you want. Pat and Tom would be great to work with. And it'll be closer to ride the bike to Monash.'

Tim and John shared a house in the foothills outside Melbourne. Tim had just finished his degree in English literature. John had always liked English and writing at school, too, but you just couldn't do everything. School and university always seemed to make you choose between science and humanities.

'What about you?' John asked. 'What're you going to do now?'

'I don't know,' Tim replied. 'Keep looking for fossils down at Inverloch, I reckon!'

They laughed. Maybe it was best to stick at what you enjoyed most. At least if you did what you loved, you'd be the best person for the job, if a job ever did turn up.

John decided to finish his degree with Pat at Monash. He was doing well enough at university to get into honours and do a small research project for his final fourth year. And after that, he could apply for a scholarship to do a doctorate where he could spend three years doing nothing but vertebrate palaeontology. It sounded perfect! And at least he wouldn't have to worry about getting a job for another few years.

John's third year flew past. He finished all his subjects, including a small research project on diprotodons at Bacchus Marsh. He was soon ready to enrol in his honours year.

Meanwhile, Tim had also been busy, going back to Inverloch and searching for more dinosaur bones. He'd found about 30 specimens, including the thigh bone of a small dinosaur.

Pat had managed to enrol Tim in a Master of Science degree at Monash, studying fossil kangaroos, even though he didn't have an undergraduate science degree.

> John's cousin **Tim Flannery** also went on to become a palaeontologist and is a well-known writer and climate change activist.

'The dinosaur work is going to be incredibly slow and time-consuming,' Pat warned John. 'It'll take a lot of time and money and volunteers. It's not great for an honours project.'

'What makes a good honours project?' asked John.

'Something specific where you already have plenty of material,' said Pat. 'And something interesting enough to publish a paper on.'

John thought back to the project on Victorian fossil fish and sharks that he'd done for the Science Talent Search while he was still at school. He remembered the strange little armoured fish he'd drawn – *Bothriolepis*.

There were hundreds of different species of *Bothriolepis* in the Devonian rocks from 370 million years ago and they were very common. The presence of one particular species allowed geologists to date the rock very precisely, which helped them explore for gas and oil.

John already had quite a collection of fossil fragments from all over Australia. Without complete skeletons, though, it was difficult to tell which fragments were which species. And which fossils were new undescribed species.

But recently, the head of Zoology at Monash, Professor James Warren, had found an incredibly rich site of Devonian fish at Mount Howitt in the highlands of Victoria. The fish had been crushed flat, leaving their imprint between layers of shale rock. Once the imprints were cleaned with hydrochloric acid, they could be filled with latex. The resulting cast showed all the details of the bones which had once lain there. These imprints of whole fish were really important for helping to identify fragments of fish from elsewhere.

John had already noticed that one of the *Bothriolepis* fish looked different from any others described.

'What about *Bothriolepis* from Mount Howitt?' he asked.

Pat nodded.

'Sounds good. There's a lot of work done on them overseas and from Gogo in Western Australia, but not in Victoria,' she said. 'That'd make a great project.'

First, John decided he need to learn more about how living armoured fish were put together.

'The pet shop has armoured fish from South America,' a friend told him. 'Might be worth a look.'

Heading into the local pet shop, John found the large, heated tanks on the back wall. In the dimly lit space, he could see suckermouth catfish lying on the bottom of the aquariums. Most modern fish had scales, but ancient fish like *Bothriolepsis* had bony plates or armour. So did the suckermouth catfish. John hoped he might learn from a modern armoured species how the bony plates fitted together.

The catfish lay with their large fins spread out like lace fans in all different patterns and colours. Their gills moved slowly in the warm water. John looked at the price tag. One hundred dollars for a fish! He could never afford that. He looked along the row. One of the fish was lying very still indeed. In fact, it was lying upside down – and its gills weren't moving.

Surely a dead fish would have to be cheaper than a live one?

'Excuse me,' John said to the shopkeeper. 'There's a dead fish in the tank out the back. Could I buy it?'

The shopkeeper stomped over to the tank.

'That fish is not dead!' he declared. 'It's just resting!'

'But it's not moving,' protested John. 'Do fish often rest upside down?'

The shopkeeper looked at the fish closely. Its eyes were milky white. He stuck his hand in and poked it.

The fish didn't move.

The shopkeeper gave the fish a shove.

The fish still didn't move.

He scooped the fish out of the water and brought it up to his face. John thought the man was going to try mouth-to-mouth resuscitation.

The shopkeeper glared at him.

'This fish is dead!' he shouted, startling all the customers in the shop. 'And it was expensive, too!'

'Yes,' agreed John, 'it *is* dead. So can I buy it?'

'What?' screamed the shopkeeper in disbelief. 'You want to buy a dead fish? What's wrong with you? Take the fish – I don't want it!'

He threw the dead fish at John, who quickly scooped it up and hurried out of the shop before anyone could blame him for the poor animal's death.

*

John finished his thesis on *Bothriolepsis* and published his first scientific paper on them, even naming three new species. Scientists had previously thought that the Australian ones were the same as

those found in Europe, but in fact, they were quite different.

One evening, John and Tim were watching David Attenborough's new TV series *Life on Earth*. Attenborough was describing fossil fish found in the cold, grey rocks of England. Suddenly, the scene changed to brilliant blue skies and a wide flat landscape. John sat up. This had to be Australia.

A small plane took off from a remote airstrip and flew over some remote ranges in the Kimberley. Attenborough explained that the sharp ridges were once a huge coral reef in a shallow sea.

'And here, I'm walking on the ancient seabed,' said Attenborough, 'turned into sandstones and mudstones. And in them are the remains of the creatures that lived in those seas.'

Attenborough stooped and picked up a smooth round rock and turned it over to show the camera.

'Here is one that I picked up a few moments ago,' he said, exposing the fossilised bony plate of a huge fish. He then showed a beautiful fragment of a skull of one of the earliest fish with true jaws.

'He made that look easy!' said Tim. 'Do you reckon he just stepped off the plane and picked that up straightaway?'

John laughed.

'Still, it's pretty amazing that we have such an important site for fish evolution right here. You'll have to go there, John.'

> When David Attenborough came to Australia in 1979 to film on **Gogo**, locals assured him there was nothing to see there. When he stepped out of the helicopter to start filming, the first stone he picked up contained the fossil he showed on air. His program brought the Gogo fossils to international attention.

'One day,' John replied. One day he'd get to Gogo in the Kimberley and see those ancient reefs for himself.

*

By the end of 1980, both John and Tim had finished their degrees and were ready to enrol in PhDs. Tim had decided to go to New South Wales to continue his work on macropods. John got an offer to go to Berkeley University in the United States.

'Berkeley would be amazing,' said Tim. 'It'd be a great opportunity.'

'I'm not sure,' John said, pushing his hand through his hair as he thought about it. 'The fossils are a bit ordinary. If I stay here, I'll have all of the Mount Howitt fish material to work on. There'll be lots of new species to describe and a chance to understand more about fish evolution.'

Fish evolution wasn't just about fish. Fish were the ancestors of all the other vertebrates like reptiles, mammals and birds – even humans. Understanding fish evolution was about understanding where all these species came from. John decided to stay in Australia.

Three years later, he had turned his schoolboy project on Victorian fossil fish into a two-volume PhD thesis. He was now Dr John Long, a qualified palaeontologist, with a wife and a baby daughter, Sarah, to support.

Professor Singleton's words echoed in his head.

'You'll never get a job as a palaeontologist.'

The hard work was only just beginning.

10

Into the West

'What do you need a car for?' asked the finance officer at the University of Western Australia, looking over her glasses.

'I need to book a four-wheel drive to get up to the Kimberley to collect fossils – probably for about six weeks,' replied John.

The woman put down her pen.

'To book one of the university cars for that length of time,' she did some quick sums on her calculator, 'will cost about five thousand dollars.'

'But that's the same as a car hire company,' protested John.

'You'll need to find some funding then,' she replied, turning back to the piles of printed spreadsheets she was working on.

John's heart sank as he left the office. His funding at the university was nowhere near enough to pay for car hire, let alone food and equipment. He needed more money if he ever wanted to get up to Gogo.

John had been lucky after finishing his PhD. With no other job options around, he applied for an Australian Research Council fellowship. There were only two of these fellowships at the time for the whole of Australia, so the chances of being successful were pretty remote. No one was more surprised than he was when he found out that he'd been awarded one.

> The **Australian Research Council** provides funding and grants for research in Australia across all areas of science and humanities, including fellowships which employ people to do research. There are other government agencies that fund medical research and defence.

The fellowship allowed him to work on some of the Gogo fossils stored at the Australian National University in Canberra before moving his growing family to Western Australia. Peter, born in Canberra, joined Sarah who had been born in Melbourne. John really needed to do some impressive research while his funding lasted in the hope that he could land a permanent job.

He needed to get to the Kimberley and see if there were any more of the amazingly preserved Gogo fossils lying around, as Attenborough had found. If he couldn't get into the field, he had no chance of continuing his career as a palaeontologist.

John set to work applying for every **grant** he could find. After a few months he marched back into the Finance Office, proudly waving a cheque for $21,000 from the National Geographic Society to buy a second-hand four-wheel drive.

'Oh, no,' said the finance officer. 'You can't buy your own car with University money. You give us the money and we'll purchase a suitable vehicle.'

'Okay,' said John, 'I need something a few years old without too many kilometres on the clock for under $20,000. Then I can use the rest to fit it out for fieldwork.'

'That's not how this works,' she said, patiently. 'First, the University only buys new vehicles.'

John was devastated. He didn't have enough money for a new four-wheel drive.

'And, once the vehicle is in the University fleet, you'll have to book it just like everyone else,' she continued. 'If it's available when you want it.'

'What's the point of that?' asked John.

'And, you'd still have to pay the rental fees,' she added.

John was shocked. It looked as if his very first major scientific grant had just vanished.

The finance officer handed the cheque back to John.

'Lucky the National Geographic Society wrote that cheque in your name,' she commented quietly, 'not the university.'

John left the office with the cheque in his hand. The grant didn't mention the university at all. It was money for his research. He quickly banked the cheque and hurried to the car yard to find just the right one to become his 'Gogomobile'.

*

A fortnight later, having said his goodbyes to his family, John drove the bright red Pajero into the car park to pick up the volunteers for the trip. The Pajero was only two years old and perfect for the rugged conditions up north.

Susan and Chris slung their backpacks into the back of the car.

'Wow, air-conditioning!' Susan exclaimed as she climbed in. 'Fancy!'

Susan was a zoology student who had been on lots of university field trips before. Chris worked in the library, but he loved exploring, so he was keen to come along for the adventure and help John out with fieldwork. On the way, they would also be joining Andy, a geologist, and Richard, an anatomy lecturer.

'None of the geology cars have air-conditioning,' agreed Chris. 'This even has FM radio and a cassette player!'

'Good shock absorbers, too,' commented Susan as they went over the car park speed hump. 'This is going to be the most comfortable field trip ever!'

'Nothing but the best for palaeos!' John said, grinning.

It took them four days to drive 2,500 kilometres north-east across central Western Australia, from Perth to Fitzroy Crossing. Fitzroy Crossing was a sprawling shanty town near the Fitzroy River. Patches of grass dotted the bare red soil beneath an occasional tree. Luckily it was winter, so not too hot or wet. They drove past tin sheds and cyclone-fenced yards filled with rusty old trucks. Doors fell off houses decaying in the damp tropical heat.

They parked in the central square enclosing the supermarket, butcher, post office and a café. After refuelling and picking up a few supplies, they quickly headed out of town to Gogo Station.

The Gogo Station homestead was an old stone house surrounded by wide verandahs and shady trees. A tall, tanned man in jeans, boots and a broad ten-gallon hat, stepped out to greet them — every inch a Kimberley cattleman. He seemed a bit suspicious of them.

'John Long,' said John, introducing himself and then the rest of the group. 'From the University of Western Australia. I wrote to you about a fossil expedition at Laidlaw Range.'

The collecting site was 100 kilometres to the east, at the far end of Gogo Station. The station had once covered millions of hectares of fertile land regularly flooded by the Fitzroy River. Without the approval of the station manager, their field trip couldn't even begin.

He looked at John with narrowed eyes under his wide hat. Then suddenly, he flashed a broad smile and held out his hand.

'Oh, yeah, I remember,' he said, crushing John's hand in his grip. 'Looking for old bones, hey? Go for it. Just don't get in the way of mustering.'

The drive east took them past rounded, ochre-coloured sandstones and jagged, grey limestones, the remnants of Permian ice-age river sands over the older Devonian marine reefs. They followed the track up a valley between the foothills. They were surrounded by prickly desert grasses, a few spindly trees and lots of rocks. The further they travelled, the tracks became narrower, splitting off into different directions. In places, they had to dodge around boulders or bounce through rock-strewn creek beds.

John squinted at the hand-drawn map he'd been given, trying to guess the right direction. They took compass bearings off landmarks and backtracked after wrong turns or valleys sliced with impassable ravines until, finally, they made it to the bottom of the Laidlaw Ranges.

Suddenly John noticed a scattering of pale tan lumps that looked like strange alien eggs in the spiky grass.

'Stop the car!' he yelled.

He leapt out with his geological hammer. There was no mistaking these rocks. These were the famous Gogo nodules. He smashed one open with his hammer and there they were: traces of broken shells inside. It was definitely the right stuff and the right place.

Between 430 and 360 million years ago, the ranges here had been a vast underwater barrier reef stretching along the coast. The fish and other marine life once living on the reef had fallen to the bottom of the seafloor when they died. The seafloor lacked oxygen and so the animals decomposed very slowly Gradually, their bodies were gently covered with **sediments** that eventually turned into limestone. So, unlike fossils elsewhere, the Gogo fossils were preserved intact and undamaged, not crushed flat.

John felt as if he was in the movie *Valley of the Gwangi* which he'd seen as a kid, where a group of cowboys discovered a lost valley of living dinosaurs. It had been decades since any scientists had been here. These nodules concealed incredible treasures and any one of them might crack open to reveal the gaping jaw of a 400-million-year-old fish.

It was getting late and they had to reach their campsite before dark. As they drove off, the setting sun lit up the grey limestone ridges with a brilliant orange-red glow. It looked as if a billion dead organisms from millions of years ago were still glowing with life.

'There it is,' said Susan, pointing to a distinctive limestone knoll in the middle of the valley. She looked at the map Andy had drawn showing how to get to his secret campsite: 'Wade Knoll. Follow the track east.'

They wound their way along a narrow track. The grass grew taller than the car on each side. Sheer cliffs closed in around them. It felt as if they were making their way to a hidden valley that time forgot.

Suddenly, they came to the opening where Andy and his assistant Mark were camped. They parked the gogomobile next to Andy's four-wheel drive and set up their tents in a circle around the campfire. The two-way radio crackled with the chatter of Indonesian fishermen offshore. They radioed their location to the Royal Flying Doctor Service and listened to the news and weather. Darkness fell suddenly as it does in the tropics and they were soon surrounded by deep shadows flickering in the campfire light beneath the brilliantly glowing carpet of the Milky Way.

The next day, they went to seek permission from the local Gooniyandi people to explore their Country and were invited to visit Galeru Gorge, a spectacular sacred site created by a creek slicing through the limestone. It was so hot that they were happy to strip off and swim the length of the gorge, dramatic cliffs rising above them while freshwater crocodiles sunned themselves on nearby banks.

Finally, they got to the serious business of fossil hunting. Over the next few days, they worked their way through unexplored patches of Gogo nodules. But it wasn't easy. The valleys often disappeared into steep ravines with nowhere to turn around, the gogomobile sometimes tilting precariously sideways on the edge of the creeks.

Whenever they needed supplies or repairs, they had to go all the way back to Fitzroy Crossing. They often had to dig the car out of rutted creek beds, and on one occasion, the trailer tray came clean off its wheelbase and had to be welded back into place.

Then one day, the car got so bogged they couldn't budge it, no matter how much they pushed or pulled or dug.

'We'll have to walk out to get help,' John said to Andy.

Leaving Chris and Susan with the car, they headed towards the highway, several hours away, navigating by map and compass across country. Flocks of zebra finches chirruped noisily in the trees as vast clouds of green and yellow budgerigars swept overhead. For a while, a rangy dingo tracked them at a distance.

The warm day turned cold and John regretted wearing only a t-shirt and shorts. When they finally reached the empty highway at nine o'clock, it was pitch-black with only the faint glow of starlight as their companion. They sat down to wait for a passing truck.

Two hours later, they finally got a lift to a nearby station, so it was past midnight before they got back to pull out the bogged car. They were all very relieved to climb into their warm sleeping bags after being out in that cold night for so many hours.

Despite the difficulties, they collected some amazing fossils. They found a beautifully preserved ray-finned fish, so detailed they could see every scale and bone. The next find was a lobe-finned fish, *Onchodus*, with a mouth full of extraordinary dagger-like teeth. Then an armoured placoderm and an unusual crustacean.

> **Ray-finned fish** are a very large group of bony fish whose fins are webbed between bony spines. Nearly 99% of all modern fish belong to this group. **Lobe-finned fish** are a different group with thick fleshy fins. There are many fossil lobe-finned species but only eight living species – two coelacanths and six lungfish.

John started filling an old 44-gallon drum with the fossils in their limestone casings. He carefully layered them between empty beer cartons and old newspapers. Once full, he sealed it up and shipped it back to Perth. There, the nodules would be soaked in a gentle acid bath to remove the limestone and reveal their fossils.

*

'John,' called Chris from across the field one morning. 'Come and look at this.'

John ran over. Sharp pointed teeth in a shiny jawbone poked out of the broken nodule.

'*Gogonasus!*' declared John, excitedly. 'I described this genus from a small snout and braincase in the geology collection in Canberra. It came from the 1967 Scottish expedition here.

If this is a complete skull or skeleton,' he added, 'it will tell us what the rest of the fish looked like, so we'll be able to identify other fossil fragments in this genus.'

'Didn't you say *Gogonasus* was the ancestor of **tetrapods**?' asked Susan.

'Could be,' answered John. 'Of all these fish, it's this one that seems to lead to the air-breathing, four-legged creatures that stepped out of the water and ultimately gave rise to all the vertebrates that live on land.'

This was an amazing place. The ancient sea floor they walked on had witnessed the moment when fish had split into two groups. One branch had evolved into all the modern scaled fish that dominate the oceans today. While the other branch evolved into the tetrapods: all the reptiles, birds, amphibians and mammals, including humans.

John held up the row of teeth embedded in the rock.

'Meet your great, great, great, great grandma!' he said, grinning.

*

Not all of John's research trips to the Kimberley went quite as smoothly.

On one trip further inland, John rang home after a week out of range, to find that everyone was frantic with worry for them. The expeditioners had noticed light planes buzzing overheard but hadn't realised that the planes were looking for a fleeing gunman who had murdered two men just across the border. A massive manhunt had been underway for the gunman who had fled straight past their campsite to Fitzroy Crossing.

Later, as they sat in the pub at Fitzroy Crossing, they heard all about how the gunman had been cornered by tactical forces in full camouflage gear.

There were explosions of tear gas, the gunman had opened fire, setting fire to the grass and starting an open gun battle with police. John was glad they hadn't known about what was happening while they were in the field!

The bush had its own dangers, too. While picking up some wood for the fire, one of John's colleagues suddenly yanked his arm away.

'What's up?' asked John, puzzled.

'Death adder,' said Terry, pointing to where John's hand had been a few moments before. John gulped. The death adder was perfectly camouflaged against the sand and wood.

Terry, an experienced wildlife handler, pinned the snake down and picked it up behind its head. It opened its jaws, dripping venom from long fangs. Beautiful, but deadly – one bite could kill you. It was a sight John would never forget!

Despite all the great discoveries John was making in the Kimberley, his fellowship money was about to run out and his third child was due to be born in a month. He urgently needed to find a new job, but there weren't any jobs for a palaeontologist in the newspapers. In desperation,

he started applying for jobs in banks and at the new Matilda Bay Brewery in Perth.

It looked as if John's career as a palaeontologist was about to end.

11

Fossils in the spotlight

The big, white Land Cruiser jumped and shuddered along the steep forest track near the border of Thailand and Burma. John clung to his seat as they swung around the tight bends.

Just as John had been about to give up on his palaeontology career, he'd had an unexpected phone call from Clive Burrett, an invertebrate palaeontologist at the University of Tasmania. Clive had a grant to work on Devonian and Silurian invertebrate fauna in south-east Asia and he needed an assistant quickly. Luckily, he'd remembered meeting John at a conference and had heard he might be looking for work.

'I've got a field trip scheduled for Thailand and Burma soon,' Clive had warned him. 'Can you make it?'

'Absolutely,' said John.

'Right, that's a deal then,' said Clive. 'And if you find any fossil fish on the trips, they're yours.'

So that's how John found himself in the back of a truck on a remote track in the Golden Triangle. The area was famous for illegal opium crops and drug gangs. Just a week earlier, some tourists had been kidnapped and killed nearby.

'Turn left up here,' said Clive to the driver. 'There's a new road being cut through.'

'Where to?' asked John.

'Somewhere in the northern mountains,' said Clive. 'There'll be fresh cuttings we can collect samples from.'

The vegetation was so thick and spiky here it was impossible to find fossil-bearing rocks, except where they had been exposed by road works. They stopped where the road sliced through the sedimentary layers of a hill.

'This'll do,' Clive said to the driver. 'We'll walk the rest of the way and you can go back to town for supplies and pick us up in an hour.'

John and Clive set to with their hand picks, chiselling off slabs of rock and inspecting them for fossils.

'Look,' said John, 'it's a shark's tooth.'

'Don't think any sharks have been described from Thailand before,' said Clive. 'Is there any more of it?'

As John turned to go back to digging, he noticed something move out of the forest. A group of roughly dressed hills tribesmen gathered around them. They had ancient rifles slung over their shoulders and they weren't smiling. Clive looked worried.

'Did you see our car go past?' asked Clive very slowly in Thai, 'Big white car. Government car – United Nations.'

He looked down the road as if he was listening for it.

'Be here in a minute,' he added.

The men didn't respond. They looked Clive and John up and down slowly. John was glad he was dressed in grubby field clothes. Tourists were often robbed for watches and cash here.

John imagined the headlines: **Fossil Fossickers Shot Dead in Drug Battle.** His blood froze. Imagine never seeing his kids again? His youngest daughter, Maddy, had only just been born, Peter was only four and Sarah had just started school. It didn't bear thinking about.

Suddenly, the men just turned away and disappeared back into the forest. A few minutes later they heard the distant sound of their approaching car.

'Phew! We better find the rest of that shark,' said John. 'I'm not coming back here!'

*

John and his family stayed in Hobart for two years, but he was soon worrying about finding the next job. It wasn't easy moving with three kids – new houses, new schools, new friends. John's work often took him a long way from home on field trips which was also hard on his family. And he was desperate to get back to working on the Gogo fossils.

If only he could find a permanent job in a museum that would let him focus on researching

Western Australian fossils. That would be just perfect.

*

'There's a letter for you,' called the office manager, as John rushed down the corridor, 'in your pigeonhole.'

'Really? Thanks!' John replied, as he spun around to go back to the mailroom. He'd only been at the museum for a few weeks and was still finding his way around.

He could hardly believe that he'd managed to land his dream job – a permanent position -- as the Curator of Vertebrate Palaeontology at the Western Australian Museum in Perth.

The letter was from Paul Foulkes, an amateur naturalist in Broome, and he had news about dinosaur footprints.

John had heard about the Broome dinosaur footprints which were found by some girl scouts walking along Gantheaume Point in the 1930s. There was a small cluster of footprints, each about 37 centimetres long, made by a medium-sized predatory dinosaur.

Paul's letter was a bombshell. He'd found *more* footprints – lots of them – and completely different from the earlier ones. This discovery was too exciting to miss. John scraped together some fieldwork funds, said goodbye to the family, and headed off on his first official museum expedition.

Paul had already been given permission from the Yawuru elders for John to visit and study the footprints on their Country. In addition to three-toed meat-eaters like the earlier footprints, there were giant sauropod footprints over *a metre* across, as well as a variety of large and small plant-eating ornithopods. Even more exciting were some stubby three-toed footprints near lopsided five-fingered handprints. John was sure that this must have been a stegosaurus – which would be the only evidence of a stegosaur in Australia.

A hundred million years ago these animals walked across a soft river flat of fine sand, clay and mud. Their footprints had baked hard in the summer sun before disappearing under layers of fine sand or silt.

John quickly got down to work, photographing, measuring and taking casts of all the imprints, noting where each footprint was located in the trackway. Individual footprints revealed the type

and size of dinosaur, but trackways revealed what the animals were doing, how they moved, ate and rested, and whether they were alone or in a family. This large collection of footprints was invaluable to palaeontologists. And they were also sacred to the local Aboriginal people, forming part of their ancestral songlines across Country.

> **Songlines** tell the history and law of the Australia's Indigenous people. The large three-toed dinosaur trackways near Broome form part of the Goolarabooloo songlines and tell the story of Marrala, the Emu Man.

After logging all the records he could, John went back to his regular work at the museum and his fish research. Then one day he got an urgent phone call from the Kimberley Land Council which represented the **Indigenous people** in the area.

'We've had a dinosaur footprint stolen up here,' the councillor said.

'Where from?' asked John.

'North of Broome.' The councillor detailed a location well-known to John.

'They chiselled the whole plate out of the rock shelf. Do you have photos of the footprints up there?

We need to know which ones have been taken and if they were valuable.'

'They're all priceless,' replied John, his heart sinking. How could someone be so selfish to steal rare fossils? But he knew why. There was always someone willing to pay a big price for illegal fossils.

The site's Indigenous custodian was furious.

'It's a sacred thing to me,' he said angrily to the reporters, 'punishable by death. If he comes to face me, I will put a spear through him and finish him.'

John's records soon proved just how damaging the theft had been. The stolen footprints belonged to the stegosaur. The only evidence that a stegosaur existed in Australia had vanished.

After investigating, the police felt sure that the fossils had already left the country. The trail went cold, but a local filmmaker was keen to see if he could find out more.

'Have they really left the country?' he asked John. 'Or are they still in someone's backyard? Don't you want to find out?'

'Of course,' said John. 'But how?'

'I know a policeman from Wyoming in the US,' he said. 'He specialises in fossil-related crimes.

He'll come and help us make a documentary, but we need you to identify the fossils.'

The museum was often involved in disputes over the ownership of fossils. This was a problem that needed more public attention.

'Okay,' John said. 'How can I help?'

Starring in a TV show and investigating international crimes wasn't what John had expected to do as a palaeontologist. Their investigations took him to London, Germany and the United States. They went undercover, posing as wealthy fossil dealers. They wired up with hidden cameras and microphones. They recorded collectors and dealers bragging about stealing fossils and illegally exporting them. They talked to convicted criminals, wealthy collectors and angry scientists. They were even stalked through dark alleys and followed by cars with tinted windows.

John was glad he'd taken up karate again. He'd finally achieved his black belt in a gruelling Sanchin exam, although he hadn't been able to walk for three days afterwards. Even so, he didn't really want to have to put these skills to the test against an armed crime gang.

But for all their efforts there was no trace of the stegosaurus footprints. Returning to Australia, they even searched for the missing footprints in someone's grave, but with no luck.

> The documentary **Dinosaur Dealers** was screened on SBS TV in Australia and John also wrote a book of the same name about his experiences.

John realised that Australia needed much better laws to protect valuable fossils and fossil sites. International fossil trading is really big business, involving fraud, theft, corruption and extortion.

*

It was still dark when the fleet of black Australian Federal Police cars came to pick John up at his house.

'There's a suspected haul of illegal fossils south of Perth,' said the officer as John got into the car. 'We think they're from China, but we need to be sure.'

The Chinese government had banned the export of many Chinese fossils and had asked the Australian government for help crack down on this crime, so the AFP was called in to investigate. John's job was to identify where the fossils came from.

When they arrived it was just like the movies. The federal police agents moved in, breaking open the doors, securing the premises. Then they showed John the warehouse full of large packing cases.

'I hope you know what you're doing,' a policewoman said. 'Without your evidence, we've got nothing.'

John opened one of the crates and looked inside. He pulled out a parcel and carefully unwrapped it from the layers of Chinese newspaper. It was a beautiful sabre-toothed cat skull and worth a fortune on the black market.

'Well, this isn't local,' he said, grimly. 'We don't get many sabre-tooths around here.'

The haul continued: dinosaur eggs, dinosaur skeletons, many fossil rhinoceros, more sabre-tooth cat skulls, exquisite fish fossils, and beautiful long-necked marine reptiles – all from some of China's most famous fossil sites.

By the end of the day, John had examined and photographed about six million dollars-worth of illegally imported fossils. He sent photos to his colleagues in China to confirm that they were indeed Chinese species.

John's evidence nailed the case for the Australian Federal Police. The newspaper packaging even told them when and where the fossils had been wrapped.

Eventually, the fossils were handed back to China at a ceremony at the Chinese Embassy in Canberra which John attended. The Chinese government thanked Australia by giving several important Chinese fossils to Australian museums.

*

It was shared reading time at a local Perth primary school. One of the mothers was reading *The Big Golden Book of Dinosaurs* to the kids. As she closed the book, she noticed that it was dedicated to the students and teachers of a primary school in Colorado for their campaign to have the stegosaurus made the official state fossil emblem.

'Why don't we have a state fossil emblem?' she asked one of the teachers, 'or any books on Australian fossils?'

Debra Parry, who taught science, agreed. It was really hard to find material for kids on all the amazing fossils in Western Australia.

'Why don't we start our own campaign for a state fossil emblem,' Debra suggested. 'Then we could learn more about the local fossils too.'

Debra contacted John at the museum to find out more about local fossils. He invited the kids into the museum to have a look for themselves. The fish from the Gogo formation were a favourite. David Attenborough had already made them famous on his TV show. But which one to choose? The children researched all the different species and ran an election, with ballot boxes, to decide. *Macnamaraspis kaprios* was their pick.

John had discovered this fossil in 1986 and had named it after a fellow palaeontologist at the museum, Ken McNamara, on his fortieth birthday. With its armoured skull and sharp teeth, it was a great example of the different fish from Gogo. The schoolkids wrote to the Premier of Western Australia, asking him to consider a state fossil emblem. The newspapers even published articles about their campaign. The Premier soon called for public submissions on the idea.

The children at Sunderland Primary School launched into action. They adopted the Gogofish as their school emblem and collected hundreds of signatures on their petition, helped by 15 other schools. They received letters of support from famous children's writers, Paul Jennings and Morris Gleitzman, and from scientists in North America, Japan, England and Germany. The Geological Society of Australia supported their choice too.

In the end there was a choice between several fossils, including stromatolites, which are the oldest fossils on earth. Amazingly, Western Australia is home to both the 3.5-billion-year-old fossils from the Pilbara as well as *living* stromatolites in Shark Bay.

But the 219-page submission by the students and teachers at the Sunderland Primary School was a clear winner. The kids and teachers and their community were ecstatic. The Gogofish became the first state fossil emblem in Australia.

> Western Australia was the first Australian state to adopt a **fossil emblem** in 1995. Other fossils emblems include the fanged fish *Madageria fairfaxi* in NSW, an ancient soft-bodied life form *Spriggina floundersi* in South Australia and a trilobite *Batocara mitchelli* in the ACT. If your state doesn't have a fossil emblem yet, why not start a campaign for one. Which fossil would you chose?

12

A cold shock and a fishy family

John looked over the bright white Antarctic landscape gleaming under a clear blue sky.

'The weather looks alright,' he said to the team leader.

Margaret looked doubtful.

'The snow's pretty thick,' she said. 'Big day yesterday and another long trek tomorrow. Think I'll catch up on some paperwork in the office.'

She pointed to her small yellow tent.

'Is it okay if I walk to that rocky outcrop?' John gestured towards some rocks a couple of hundred metres away.

'Just be careful,' she replied. 'You know how fast the weather can turn.'

'I'll be extra careful,' he said, 'but if I'm not back by 6 o'clock send out a search party.'

This wasn't John's first trip to Antarctica. The great white continent had once been covered in thick Jurassic forests before it froze over about 134 million years ago. It was a palaeontologist's treasure trove. But it was so hard to get to and everything depended on the weather.

John's first trip to Antarctica had been completely unfruitful. After exhaustive training for the trip in New Zealand and an uncomfortable flight down in an Army troop transport plane, John found himself stuck at the base due to bad weather and unable to visit the sites that he could see in the distance.

But this time things were different. They'd already been out in the field for a month and found several new species, even new genera, of placoderms, sharks and bony fish. Now they had to wait for the C130 Hercules military aircraft to schedule their pick-up from the nearby glacier. John was determined not to waste a minute.

He filled his thermos with hot water and the obligatory orange flavouring. His backpack was full of snacks – chocolate, muesli bars, biscuits, cheese and dried apples. He put on his heavy-weather gear – a one-piece yellow bunny suit, two layers of gloves and two pairs of thick socks.

'Bye,' he called to Margaret. 'I'll just go for a quick squiz and be back soon.'

Famous last words!

John headed off and soon found himself wading through thigh-deep snow. It was hard work. He looked back at the camp. The two yellow tents, four wooden sledges and two bright orange toboggans looked tiny beneath the dark brooding mountains.

Silence closed in around him except for the snow squeaking under his boots and the occasional loud crack in the ice. He pushed on towards the green-grey layers of sandstone and shale ahead. Now the snow was up to his waist.

Suddenly, John's foot stepped into thin air. His other foot slipped after it. He was falling under the snow!

He thrashed his arms about wildly, trying to grab onto something. Fortunately, his large backpack wedged itself into the deep snow, halting his fall. But his feet still waved free beneath him, into a hidden abyss he couldn't even see.

Gasping for breath, his heart racing, John hauled himself sideways, wriggling, face first in the snow and ice to move away from the chasm. Finally, his feet gripped into the snow and he was able to crawl away from the edge... He gasped to catch his breath before turning around to see the hole he'd nearly fallen into. It was a dark-blue bottomless pit.

John shivered. He'd been literally one step away from a sudden frozen death. Plenty of explorers had died falling into hidden crevasses in Antarctica. What if he'd never seen his family again? He had to get to safety. He crawled further away, carefully feeling each step until he reached the rocks and could pull himself onto a reassuringly solid sandstone ledge.

Taking a big swig of warm orange cordial and a bite of chocolate to calm himself, he promptly burst into tears.

After a while, he wiped the salty ice off his face. He'd made it this far, so he might as well look for fossils. To his left, were some promising-looking rocks – he just had to clamber across the steep bank of snow in between.

Putting **crampons** onto his boots, John checked he had a firm foothold and secured his next step with his ice pick, lowering himself into the chest-deep snow.

He had nearly reached the rocky outcrop when he noticed small pieces of snow whizzing past. When he looked up the slope, a great wall of snow was plunging towards him. An avalanche!

John turned his back as the avalanche hit with full force. He tumbled down the slope as the snow buried him.

When the snow finally stopped, John looked up. He was buried up to his neck. Luckily, the snow was still soft so he carefully dug his way out.

With his heart pounding, he clambered onto the rocks nearby and sat frozen to the spot for some time. Forget the fossils, he thought, it was time to get home safely. He headed back to camp, careful to avoid the hole he'd nearly fallen in. By the time he arrived back, the three-hour trip felt like a lifetime.

The next day, one of the other camp members went out with a long pole, to test for crevasses on

John's route. Not only did he find the one John had fallen into, but he found that John had also crossed seven other crevasses on the way, saved only by a thin bridge of ice.

Antarctica might be a great place for fossils, but it was no place for the faint-hearted!

*

Perth had been an important base for John for many years. He'd built a successful career as a palaeontologist at the Western Australian Museum. As well as the Gogo research and Antarctica, he'd led three expeditions to the Nullarbor Caves to collect megafauna along with palaeontologists from Flinders University. He'd described 20 new species of fish, marine reptiles and even a dinosaur, and enjoyed writing lots of books for kids and adults.

It hadn't always been overseas adventures and fossil hunts, though. His family was always a very important part of his life. So after his marriage broke up, John had to learn how to parent on his own when the kids came to stay with him in his apartment in central Perth. He loved taking them into the museum with him and on field trips.

They'd had lots of fun together caving, fossil hunting, digging up diprotodons and sharing stories. He'd even written a children's book for them, based on a story he'd told them at bedtime.

'Remember that time we crossed the Fortescue River?' said Peter over dinner one night.

Sarah rolled her eyes, 'Oh yes, "we'll be fine," Dad said.'

'The river was so high, none of the other cars would attempt it, but Dad did,' exclaimed Maddy. 'There was water over the bonnet!'

'And when we got to the other side, remember what that bloke said?' added Peter.

He put on a slow country drawl.

'"Didn't think you were gunna make it, mate."'

'"Coulda used that bridge over there!"' Maddy added, hooting with laughter.

'I don't know why you have to keep telling that story,' said John.

'What about our great trip up to the Kimberley?' said Heather. 'After you won the Eureka Prize. That was fun.'

John had met Heather when she was working on exhibitions for the WA Museum in 2001. When

John won the $10,000 Eureka Prize for the promotion of science, he used the money to pay for an expedition to Gogo. This time Heather, as well as Peter and Maddy, who were still at school then, were able to come with him.

'And I found a huge fossil fish!' declared Maddy. *Eastomanosteus calliaspis* was a large predatory lungfish. Maddy's specimen was one of the few known complete fossils found.

'We've all found fossils,' Peter reminded them. 'What about my *Gogosteus sarahae* specimen?'

'Which I named for Sarah, in 1994,' John said, smiling at his eldest daughter, who'd missed that Gogo trip because of university.

'Well, some of us are still waiting for our fossils to be named after us, you know,' declared Heather pointedly.

Heather had also found a fossil on the trip. John didn't think there was much in the nodule, but he put it in the acid bath, anyway. Heather was thrilled when a huge lungfish jaw emerged. John had promised he'd name it after her if it was a new species. Unfortunately, as more of the fish appeared, John recognised the species. It was

Holodipterus longi – a species that a colleague had already named after John!

'That was rigged,' declared Heather. 'I'm still waiting for my fish!'

'Well, it might not be a new species, but it might be a new genus. It's very different from the other holodontid species,' John said. 'I promise, if it is, I'll name the genus after you.'

'You'd better!' said Heather, laughing.

> In 2020 John completed the research on the holodontid lungish from Gogo and established a new genus. The lungfish Heather found is now called **Robinsondipterus longi**, which combines both Heather and John's last names.

*

After 15 years in Perth, it was time for a change. John took up a new job as Head of Sciences back at Museum Victoria where he was in charge of all the collections that had inspired him as a child.

John enjoyed being back in his home state. He organised field trips to central Queensland, to the south coast of New South Wales as well as back to Mount Howitt, where his research first began. Despite lots of leeches in the wet forests, he had an enthusiastic band of volunteers. The Head of Research, Robin Hirst, and the Director of the Museum, Patrick Green, both joined in. By opening up new fossil sites in the black shaly rock, they found out a lot more about Victorian lungfish.

In 2005 he took another team back to Gogo and a new team member, Tim Senden from the Australian National University, found an almost complete Gogonasus, right down to the tip of its tail. It took four months for the fossil to emerge from the acid bath.

'Look at these **spiracles**,' said John to Tim. He pointed to the holes on the top of the skull. 'And these pectoral fins – aren't they amazing!'

Tim agreed. 'I've run the analysis through the new software. This fish has so many similarities with early tetrapods it can't be a coincidence.'

For many years there had been much debate about the origin of tetrapods, which include all the land-dwelling vertebrates. Most people agreed that one of the fish had moved onto land, developed legs and the ability to breath air. Fish were the ancestors of all land-dwelling vertebrates, including humans. But which fish?

Some scientists thought it was the coelacanth. Others argued for lungfish. Both of these fish are still found in oceans and rivers today and are very similar to fossil species from millions of years ago.

The Gogonasus fossil had many similarities to early tetrapods, including holes in its skull for nostrils and ears. The bones in its fins are very similar to the bones found in human fingers. John had always been interested in how Devonian fish evolved and adapted, but he'd never realised how much his work revealed where humans had come from.

They sent their paper to the best scientific journal in the world, *Nature*. They heard straight back. They'd publish immediately. When the paper came out, the newspapers went wild.

'Gogofish rewrites evolution!' the headlines blared.

John was astonished. He'd never had so much publicity for his research before. Suddenly, everyone seemed to think that ancient Devonian fish were as interesting as he did. Although not all the journalists got their facts right. Sometimes he cringed at the things they got wrong. If only they would check first!

A lot had changed in palaeontology since John first started. There was a lot of work on Australian vertebrate fossils now. Fossils of Australian dinosaurs had been very rare but now large dinosaurs were being found across inland Queensland, including fearsome megaraptors like *Australovenator wintonensis* and massive titanosaurs like *Australotitan cooperensis*. There were new megafauna discoveries in Naracoorte and the Nullarbor Caves, Miocene mammals from Alcoota in the Northern Territory and fossilised ancient whales from Port Phillip Bay, where John used to hunt for fossils as a child. Palaeontology was moving fast.

*

'What do you think of that tail section?' asked John.

Kate Trinajstic, an expert in soft tissue fossil preservation, had flown all the way from Western Australia to help John with this fish. She looked at the delicate pile of tiny white bones in the white cardboard box in front them.

'It's hard to see with the rock still attached,' she replied. 'Let's have a closer look.'

They had been taking turns examining the tiny fish under the binocular microscope and describing it. It may have been tiny, but the fish had an amazingly well-preserved head and braincase. Now they only had the rather boring tail end of the fish to go.

'I think we should give it another quick soak – just for an hour or so,' John said. 'Then we'll be able to see all the bones clearly.'

They waited as the material started to gently fizz and dissolve.

'Next big paper coming up,' joked Kate, as she went back to her desk, 'about a tiny fish with a beautiful braincase.'

As John carefully lifted the fish from the chemical bath, he was pleased to see the bones were much clearer.

Then he noticed something else.

'What's that?' he muttered to himself. A pile of tiny bones lay jumbled together just before the tail.

'Could that be an embryo, do you think?' he asked Kate.

Kate looked carefully through the microscope.

'Well, that looks like an umbilical cord to me,' she replied, pointing to a small ropey structure twisted nearby the pile of bones.

John whistled.

'Really?' he said. 'I think we might be getting a big paper, after all.'

Most fish lay eggs, but just a few – like guppies and sharks – give birth to live young. John had never heard of a fossilised fish pregnancy before – and certainly not from 400 million years ago.

'We need to rule out the possibility that it's just dinner, first,' said Kate.

'It's got the same placoderm tooth plates and the head shape is the same too. It's definitely the same species,' replied John. 'Could have been eating the same species, though.'

They looked at the position of the tiny fish. It wasn't anywhere near the gut area, but lay near the reproductive organs.

'There's no damage to the scales or bones, either. I don't think it was eaten,' said Kate.

'I think we need to scan this one, John,' she added. 'Let me take it back to Perth and have a closer look.'

Techniques for studying fossils were changing fast. When John first started, fossils took months or even years of painstaking preparation before they could be studied. But now palaeontologists could use high resolution computer tomography or **CT scanners** to see features not previously visible at all.

> Even more recently, **synchrotrons** are used to scan fossils even before they removed from the rock. These football field-sized particle accelerators spin and deflect tiny high energy electrons at high speed until they emit an incredibly bright light. The light is so bright it scans through rock, revealing incredible details, even soft tissue, like organs, muscles and even nerves.

Kate managed to separate the delicate baby fish from its tiny mother. Then she coated parts of it in a fine layer of carbon and then gold to photograph even more detail. It was painstaking work, but she confirmed that the twisted ropey structure around the baby fish was definitely an umbilical cord.

'We've found the motherfish, Kate,' John declared. 'It's a new species too – and I know just who we should name this one after.'

The news of the Gogo 'motherfish' was an international sensation. It was published in *Nature* and announced via a live satellite feed from a grand gala dinner at the newly opened Royal Institute in Adelaide to guests at the newly renovated Royal Institute in Britain. Not only were leading scientists from all over the world present, but also David Attenborough himself as well as the Queen.

When John, Kate and the team named the species *Materpiscus attenboroughi* after the man who had brought the Gogo fossils to international attention, David Attenborough was delighted.

John realised that he wasn't just studying fossil fish anymore. He was looking at the origins of modern life on earth – the very things that had made humans the way they are. From fingers and toes to legs and breathing air, to giving birth to live young – these fish show us where we come from and why we take the shape we do.

13

Life in LA

The track was wet, steep and slippery. John and Heather pulled themselves up the side of the mountain on the chains attached to the rocks.

'Whose idea was it to climb a mountain on our holiday?' asked Heather, puffing.

'It'll be worth it,' said John, helping her up the last step. 'Nearly there.'

Mt Warning was a magma plug from an ancient volcano. Its steep pointed cone rose just south of the Queensland border in the Lamington National Park.

'Just look at that,' exclaimed John as they finally reached the viewing platform on the top. The view across the Great Dividing Range was breathtaking.

'You're right,' said Heather. 'It was worth it. Sometimes you've got to kick yourself out of your comfort zone and try something new.'

Heather had a point, thought John. He'd been at Museum Victoria for five years. John's research was going extraordinarily well and everything was good. But there were no big adventures on the horizon. Maybe it was time for new opportunities?

'What about America?' John suggested. 'There's so much happening over there in palaeontology. Do you think you could live there?'

'Hell, yes,' said Heather, her eyes lighting up with excitement. 'Let's do it!'

When they got back from their holidays, John spotted a job advertised at the Natural History Museum in Los Angeles. This museum had the third biggest natural history collection in the country with over 35 million objects.

'Not just natural history, either,' added Heather as she looked over his shoulder. 'It has an amazing art collection as well as artefacts from Indigenous American cultures.'

'Apparently, it has one of the first biplanes to fly around the world,' John added. 'Well, no harm in applying.'

A few weeks later, John got a phone call.

'Looks like we're going on a trip to Los Angeles,' he said to Heather, grinning.

Their first trip in March was a whirlwind. They drove around the city on the wrong side of the road. Los Angeles was very busy compared to Perth or Melbourne. They loved all the cultural activities and the beautiful beaches.

In July, the museum flew John over again for two days of interviews, giving talks and meeting board members and trustees.

Afterwards, he rang Heather from LA.

'I got the job! What should I say?'

'Yes, of course, Mr. Vice President of Research and Collections!' replied Heather. 'Los Angeles, here we come!'

When John arrived, the vast central halls of the museum were empty. They were undergoing a major refurbishment and overseeing this would be one of John's major tasks. Developing, planning and installing such big exhibitions wasn't just about choosing objects, preparing them for display, developing the stories to tell, or finding new ways to tell them. It was also about managing the people doing all that work. John knew it was going to be a big job, but maybe not just *how* big.

'So, the records say this is in a storehouse downtown,' said John to one of the collection managers, as they tracked down an object for display. Only a few of the museum's millions of objects were ever on display. Most were stored in warehouses all over Los Angeles. 'Can you go and have a look for it?'

The collection manager shook her head.

'I haven't been to that warehouse in years. It's not safe,' she replied. 'Josh can go. He can take Miguel with him.'

John frowned. He didn't always understand the tensions between staff.

'Josh has only been here a few months,' John pointed out. 'He's much more junior than you.'

'But he gets paid more,' said the collection manager, bitterly.

'That can't be right,' exclaimed John. 'You've been here ten years longer and have a more senior role with much more responsibility.'

She shrugged.

'That's how it works here,' she said. 'Our pay stays the same. So, people who started more recently often get better pay.'

'That's not fair,' said John. 'In Australia, your pay goes up with experience and promotion.'

'Our pay is all over the place here,' said the collection manager. 'Junior assistants get paid more than senior curators. Doesn't matter how much work we do or how much experience we have. And those warehouses are not safe to work in, anyway. Staff can't go there on their own.'

John looked into the spreadsheets on his computer. She was right. The pay rates were a nightmare. And so were the warehouses. Some of them leaked and flooded, others weren't even air-conditioned. They certainly weren't good for the priceless collections – and their rental was costing the museum a fortune.

One evening at a museum function, John found himself talking to one of the trustees, who was a property developer. He was complaining to John about the slow rental market.

'I have huge factories lying empty. No one is interested in renting.'

'How big are they?' asked John, quickly running some mental calculations. 'Do they have climate control?'

Before long, John had worked out a deal. He could move all the museum collections into one custom-fitted facility with all the modern conveniences, locked into a long-term contract, for less than the price of all the current substandard warehouses scattered across town. And once he'd done that, he might even have enough in the budget to make sure everyone was paid fairly.

*

The new Dinosaur Hall at the Los Angeles Natural History Museum opened in 2011 with great fanfare. It was no longer filled with dusty bones on rows of tables as it had been in the past. Now the exhibition brought the fossils to life, with reconstructions, soundscapes and audiovisuals. The latest scientific knowledge about these amazing creatures and their prehistoric worlds was on display.

The centrepiece was the *Tyrannosaurus rex* growth series – although everyone called it the *T. rex* family. It featured a skeleton of the youngest

known baby *T. rex* along with a rare adolescent and one of the most complete skeletons of an adult T. rex in the world.

With over 300 fossils and 20 complete mounts of dinosaurs and marine reptiles, there was plenty for everyone: a massive triceratops, stegosaurus, allosaurus, and a long-necked plesiosaur, *Mamenchisaurus* that snaked through the gallery. It was like standing in an illustration from one of John's childhood books on American dinosaurs.

> Both North America and Australia had a vast **inland sea** in the time of the dinosaurs filled with prehistoric marine creatures like giant sharks and plesiosaurs like **Mamenchisaurus**.

But even so, John missed his own research and the Australian fossils he had spent so much time studying. It had been a big challenge – a huge job – being in charge of a major museum department. But what he really wanted to be doing – what he always wanted to do – was to be digging up new fish fossils and working out what new and amazing things they could teach him about the evolution of life on earth.

'Time to go home, now?' asked Heather as she came up behind him.

'Yes,' said John, 'I think it is.'

14

Future of fossils

It was strange, coming back to Australia after the busy whirlwind of life in Los Angeles. Having spent most of his life working in museums, John took up a position as Professor of Palaeontology at Flinders University in Adelaide. Flinders University had a fantastic palaeontology team. John had already worked with many of them on the Nullarbor cave fossils.

Being at a university meant being part of a much bigger team, with lots of students and more facilities. There were people working on all sorts of different aspects of fossils, like ecologists and botanists, even chemists and engineers. There were specialised laboratories too, for doing chemical analyses on the fossils, or dating them using **radioactive isotopes**. Now they have a large CT scanner for the fossils.

John did two further field trips to Antarctica, this time reaching the remote Transantarctic Mountains. The researchers were helicoptered onto the site where they lived and often dug for fossils, inside their tiny self-contained tents pinned to the mountainside.

> The **Transantarctic Mountains** stretch from one side of the continent to the other, separating east from west. They are the last place on Antarctica to have had trees and contain important fossils, including fish, dinosaurs and plants, from a time when Antarctica connected Australia and South America.

*

In 2014 John had the great honour of being the first Australian ever to be elected president of the international Society of Vertebrate Palaeontologists.

One of the best things about being president of an international society was being able to highlight

Australian fossils. For a lot of northern hemisphere scientists, Australia was a long way away. They weren't used to travelling far for conferences. John was determined to convince them that Australia was worth the visit.

'There's never been a Vertebrate Palaeontology Society conference held in the southern hemisphere,' his Australian colleagues had said. 'They'll never agree.'

'They'll argue about it endlessly,' added someone else.

'Well, let's just put it to a vote then,' John told them. How many members would want to come to Australia for the next conference?

Turned out, most of them did. It was pretty amazing to finally be able to show so many international palaeontologists all the great work being done in Australia. They had the conference in Brisbane and John managed to arrange a fantastic field trip to Gogo as well.

But not all the local news was so positive.

'Have you heard about the Beaumaris development?' asked Erich, a curator from Museum Victoria who worked on fossil whales. 'They want to build a marina right over the top of the site.'

John remembered sitting on that beach as a kid and putting his hand on a five-million-year-old fossilised tiger shark tooth.

'They already covered up part of it in the 1960s with a car park!' John said. 'It's public land, not private. When this first came up ten years ago we had over two thousand palaeontologists from 100 countries write in to oppose the plan.'

'You never know when another discovery like *Pelagornis* or *Livyatan* is going to turn up on a site like that,' Erich added.

> **Pelagornis** was a giant bony-toothed seabird with a wingspan of over seven metres. The only Australian record of this species was found at Beaumaris in 2004. **Livyatan** was a giant sperm whale. A *Livyatan* tooth measuring 30 cm long was found at Beaumaris in 2016 by a local resident.

John rubbed his forehead. It was a constant battle to protect fossils from development and poor legislation. It seemed wrong that something so valuable that had survived for millions of years should be destroyed for a car park or a house.

'Fossils fuel the economy,' said Erich. 'Just a shame we burn them in our cars instead of learning from them.'

> Coal, crude oil and natural gas are known as '**fossil fuels**' because they were formed from the fossilised remains of the great Jurassic forests that once sustained the dinosaurs. Because of their organic origins, they contain huge amounts of carbon, which are released into the atmosphere when burnt, contributing to global warming and climate change.

*

That Christmas while visiting family in Melbourne, John took a walk along Beaumaris beach. He remembered what the famous American biologist, George Gaylord Simpson, had said when it was threatened with development in the 1960s.

'The scientific value of that area at Beaumaris is very great. I am sure that this is appreciated by many Australians and am confident that it will be taken into account in planning for the future there,' wrote the Harvard professor.

John knew that lots of Australians appreciated the beach cliffs and their fossils. There had been a vocal public campaign against the marina development and the proposal was finally shelved in February 2019. The site was safe again – for the moment.

He watched a small girl pick up a fossil sea urchin and run back to her father to show it to him.

What was it about dinosaurs and prehistoric animals that fascinated kids? John wondered. He thought back to how his mother had told him stories about fairies, giants and other mythical monsters. And then one day, he'd discovered dinosaurs – real monsters, not imaginary ones.

It was about change and time and imagination, John thought. It was about being able to imagine your own world being completely different from the way it is now. It was about imagining the place where you are standing right now, being a lush rainforest with giant pine trees and ferns. Or the bottom of an icy ocean. Or imagining the world without humans, without mammals, or birds or flowers.

And there was still so much more work to do, thought John. Not just the new species still waiting to be identified in the fossils he'd already collected from Gogo and Antarctica, but the big questions

– how did the human body evolve and when did arms, legs and teeth first appear?

There were so many new developments in science too, with all the high-tech machinery. Palaeontologists no longer just used a rock pick and a bucket of vinegar to prepare their fossils. Now they used synchrotrons and neutron beams to look for information in fossils that couldn't even be seen before. Palaeontology might be the study of ancient bones but it was very much a science of the future.

The small girl ran back to the rock pool with her bucket, collecting more treasures from the oceans of the past and present.

Perhaps she had a new species or a rare fossil tooth in her bucket? Perhaps it would inspire her to join the next generation of palaeontologists. What would that be like, John wondered. Maybe she wouldn't just be studying life on earth, but going on space missions to study the fossils of other planets? Who knew what further secrets of the past the future might hold?

All John knew was that he felt incredibly lucky to be spending his life studying the past and uncovering these strange and remarkable lost worlds.

Glossary

- **Crampons** – spikes that are attached to shoes to help climbing and walking through snow and ice.
- **CT scanner** – a computerised tomography scanner used to take a series of very detailed X-rays through a body or object to show what is inside.
- **Diprotodon** – a giant marsupial megafauna that lived in Australia more than 60,000 years ago.
- **Extinct** – a type of life form that has no living members in existence today.
- **Fossils** – the remains or traces of ancient organisms which have been preserved in rocks. Can include bones, footprints, plants, insects and soft tissue like feathers.
- **Geologist** – scientists who study the material that makes up the earth and other planets and the processes that shape the earth.
- **Indigenous people** – also call themselves First Nations people or Aboriginal people as they are the first people to have lived in a place.
- **Living fossil** – a living species that looks very similar to a fossil species that lived a long time ago.

- **Palaeontologist** – a scientist who studies any kind of prehistoric life except for modern humans whereas archaeologists are scientists who study the prehistory of modern humans.
- **Radioactive Isotopes** – are unstable atoms that slowly and regularly change over time. They are used for dating rocks, human made objects and fossils.
- **Sediments** – are small particles often of eroded volcanic rocks that form mud, sand or gravel. They often cover fossils, and form layers of sedimentary rocks.
- **Spiracles** – an opening on the outside of an animal to help it breathe
- **Tetrapods** – all animals with four limbs including living reptiles, amphibians, birds and mammals as well as extinct species like dinosaurs.
- **Vertebrae** – the interlocking bones of the spine or backbone

About Danielle Clode

Danielle Clode grew up on a boat sailing around Australia with her parents and her cat. She has worked as a zookeeper, in museum collections and feeding giant fish at an underwater observatory.

She studied at Adelaide University before doing her zoology doctorate at Oxford University studying seabirds in Scotland. She is now an Associate Professor of Writing at Flinders University in Adelaide.

Danielle has written many award-winning nonfiction science books about bushfires, sailing ships, killer whales and nature. She has written three books on Australian fossils including *Prehistoric Giants: The Megafauna of Australia*, *Prehistoric Marine Life of Australia's Inland Sea* and *Australia's Amazing Fossils: From Dinosaurs to Diprotodons*.

www.ingramcontent.com/pod-product-compliance
Lightning Source LLC
LaVergne TN
LVHW032010070526
838202LV00059B/6378